Years ago when I read the first version of *The Power of Hope* (*Tell Your Heart to Beat Again*), I received such revelation and inspiration on that one small but powerful word: *hope*. Dutch's new, revised book carries even more! Through the stories and teachings in the book Dutch has given us the tools to choose hope. No matter what life brings to us, we can recalibrate our hearts and set ourselves on a course to trust God, receive, and walk in hope.

—Pastor Beni Johnson
Bethel Church, Redding, CA
Author of *The Happy Intercessor*

Essayist Joseph Addison once said, "Three grand essentials to happiness in this life are something to do, something to love, and something to hope for." Hope is the immune system of the human soul. It is critical to staying in a place of contending and overcoming in these last days. My friend Dutch Sheets has written a prophetic and timely book. In *The Power of Hope* Dutch addresses heaven's ultimate remedy for counteracting hell's ultimate resistance for modern-day believers who may be struggling to believe. This book is profound yet easy to read, and it will give you an anointed adrenaline injection of inspiration to rise up when everything seems to be falling apart. I highly recommend this well-written book on hope from a general of the faith. You will not be disappointed!

—@RevSeanSmith
Director of Sean Smith Ministries/
Pointblank Intl.
Author of *Prophetic Evangelism* and
I Am Your Sign

Dutch Sheets, my dear friend, fellow intercessor for America, and favorite author, is not one of those starry-eyed optimists who refuse to see evil. No, he is one who has been hit with obstacles and disappointments on every side, yet because of his faith and experience in God, he thunders in this book, "Darkness shall not prevail, for God holds your history in His hands and He will not fasten your soul to a dead-end vision!" Throw off the counsel of despair; hope remains, and hope rumbles onward.

—Lou Engle
Visionary and cofounder, TheCall

In recent years I have experienced many deep wounds and setbacks—as a person, as a pastor, and as a preacher of God's Word.

In this increasingly negative world dreams are dashed, hope deferred, and relationships are often strained and broken. As a result, I often have secretly yearned for personal, spiritual encouragement. Recently just one of the illustrative stories and chapters in this book brought deep healing and encouragement to my soul. Dutch Sheets has penned his greatest masterpiece in this book. Destined to be a Christian classic, *The Power of Hope* will speak to every believer's heart.

—HARRY R. JACKSON JR.
SENIOR PASTOR OF HOPE CHRISTIAN
CHURCH IN BELTSVILLE, MD
PRESIDENT OF HIGH IMPACT LEADERSHIP
COALITION
PRESIDING BISHOP OF THE INTERNATIONAL
COMMUNION OF EVANGELICAL CHURCHES

It is an honor to call Dutch Sheets a spiritual father, and it is a great joy to recommend this much-needed discourse on hope. I did not realize how hope deficient I was after returning from a combat deployment with a Special Operations unit in Afghanistan. This book reawakened dreams gone dormant. Dutch's insights, when prayerfully considered and acted upon, have the power to move anyone's heart from despair to expectancy.

—WILLIAM J. OSTAN, JD, MPP

THE

POWER

of

hope

DUTCH SHEETS

BEST-SELLING AUTHOR OF *INTERCESSORY PRAYER*

THE
POWER
of
hope

CHARISMA HOUSE

Most CHARISMA HOUSE BOOK GROUP products are available at special quantity discounts for bulk purchase for sales promotions, premiums, fund-raising, and educational needs. For details, write Charisma House Book Group, 600 Rinehart Road, Lake Mary, Florida 32746, or telephone (407) 333-0600.

THE POWER OF HOPE by Dutch Sheets
Published by Charisma House
Charisma Media/Charisma House Book Group
600 Rinehart Road
Lake Mary, Florida 32746
www.charismahouse.com

Library of Congress Cataloging-in-Publication Data:
Sheets, Dutch.
  [Tell your heart to beat again]
  The power of hope / Dutch Sheets.
      pages cm
  Rev. ed. of: Tell your heart to beat again. c2002.
  Includes bibliographical references.
  ISBN 978-1-62136-632-4 (trade paper) -- ISBN 978-1-62136-633-1 (e-book)
  1. Hope--Religious aspects--Christianity. I. Title.

  BV4638.S44 2014
  234'.25--dc23

                                    2013040499

Portions of this book were previously published as
Tell Your Heart to Beat Again by Regal Books, ISBN
0-8307-3078-8, copyright © 2002.

20 21 22 23 24 — 9 8 7 6 5
Printed in the United States of America

CONTENTS

INTRODUCTION

As I write this, I'm sitting on my back porch, drawing inspiration from an amazing picture of hope. It's a tree in my backyard that I named The Hope Tree. I gave it that name because it used to be dead—or so the previous homeowners thought.

I remember talking with the former owner when I was considering purchasing the house. He told me that not only had the tree died, but he had cut it down. There was nothing left but a stump! It doesn't get much deader than that!

"Then I put in the sprinkler system," said the man. "I placed one of the sprinkler heads next to the stump, *and the tree grew back.*"

I stood next to him looking at the tree. It was not a wannabe tree consisting of two or three small sprigs, mind you, but a complete tree. Immediately I thought about a scripture where God talks about this never-say-die kind of tree:

> For there is hope for a tree, when it is cut down, that it will sprout again, and its shoots will not fail. Though its roots grow old in the ground, and its stump dies in the dry soil, at the scent of water it will flourish and put forth sprigs like a plant.
>
> —JOB 14:7–9

Why had this passage from Job come to mind so quickly? Amazingly at that time I had been encouraging myself with these exact verses from Job as I prayed for America. "You can revive America's destiny and cause us to be great again, Lord," I prayed often.

Imagine my shock as I looked at the tree before me, the perfect picture of the scriptures I had been standing on. "Sold!" I said. "I hope Ceci likes the house because I'm buying it!" That tree is now my daily reminder of the validity and power of audacious hope.

Like me, many people in this season are looking for hope. Life can be difficult, at times brutal. The struggling economy is stealing jobs and destroying the dreams of many; diseases seem to have multiplied, ravaging the health of some and taking the lives of others; our kids cut themselves and shoot their classmates; our government is broken and refuses to reform; and the entire world, it seems, is filled with unrest and war.

Stumps abound.

Fear and disillusionment seem to be winning. People everywhere are looking for hope, which is why I've written this book. It is actually a rewrite of a book I released in 2002. I have changed much, making it better and easier to read. I've also added a section at the end of each chapter that invites you to REFLECT, APPLY, and PRAY the power of hope into your life. Use the journal pages in the back of the book to record your thoughts as you spend time in the closing pages of each chapter.

The information this new edition contains will water your soul and awaken hope. As it does, I believe you will live again—just like my tree. Hope will enable you to overcome the pain of your loss, the stigma of your shame, and the paralyzing power of fear.

Never underestimate the power of hope!

The Old Testament word for *hope* has the connotation of a cord, used as an attachment; the New Testament calls it "an anchor of the soul" (Heb. 6:19). Hope will become your lifeline, your stabilizer.

You are not at the mercy of life's unpredictable

winds and currents; your storm won't destroy you. You will win. Through the power of hope and its ability to connect you to God, your song will be restored and you will sing again.

The great poet Emily Dickinson captured the sustaining power of hope in one of her beautiful poems:

> Hope is the thing with feathers
> That perches in the soul
> And sings the tunes without the words
> And never stops at all.[1]

Don't stop singing, my friend. We need your song.

Chapter One

GET BUSY LIVIN'

IN 1965 DURING a family reunion in Florida, a grandmother woke everyone at 2:00 a.m., issuing orders to get empty Coke bottles, corks, and paper. "I've received a message from God," she said. "People must hear His Word." She wrote verses on the paper while the grandchildren bottled and corked them. Then everyone deposited over two hundred bottles into the surf at Cocoa Beach.

People contacted and thanked her for the scriptures throughout the years. She died in November 1974. The next month the last letter arrived.

Dear Mrs. Gause,
I'm writing this letter by candlelight. We

no longer have electricity on the farm. My husband was killed in the fall when the tractor overturned. He left eleven young children and myself behind. The bank is foreclosing, there's one loaf of bread left, there's snow on the ground, and Christmas is two weeks away. I prayed for forgiveness before I went to drown myself. The river has been frozen over for weeks, so I didn't think it would take long. When I broke the ice, a Coke bottle floated up. I opened it, and with tears and trembling hands, I read about hope. Ecclesiastes 9:4.

"But for him who is joined to all the living there is hope, for a living dog is better than a dead lion."

You went on to reference other scriptures: Hebrews 7:19; 6:18; John 3:3. I came home and read my Bible and now I'm thanking God for the message. We're going to make it now. Please pray for us, but we're all right.

May God bless you and yours.

A Farm in Ohio[1]

How did this life-saving Coke bottle make a nine-year journey all the way from Cocoa Beach, Florida, to a river in Ohio? Not just any river, mind you, but the *right* river, near the *right* farm, at the *right* time.

I can almost hear the "Mrs. Gause Coke Bottle Angel Patrol" heaving a sigh of relief when the last message of hope was delivered nine years after it had been sent. And I can imagine God's explanation to the angels: "This last one will be a Christmas present, much like the first one I delivered to hopeless humans two thousand years ago."

Coke bottles were transformed into hope bottles—three of the four verses in the bottle were about hope. Interesting. The bottles didn't contain verses regarding power, miracles, or even provision, all of which this lady desperately needed. Why? Because those things are produced *after* we hope. The demoralizing power of hopelessness paralyzes the soul; hopeless hearts can't reach out in faith.

Hope is to the heart what seeds are to the earth. Without hope life is sterile, unfruitful. Without it dreams won't be conceived; destinies won't be realized. Hope is powerful because it is the starting line, the genesis, the launch pad. It is, in fact, the incubator where faith is formed: "Faith is the substance of things *hoped* for," God tells us (Heb. 11:1, KJV, emphasis added). If there is no hope for the future, there will be no faith to face it—let alone build it.

GET BUSY LIVIN' OR GET BUSY DYIN'

In the movie *The Shawshank Redemption* Andy (played by Tim Robbins) and Red (played by Morgan Freeman) are both serving life sentences for murder.[2] Red was guilty; Andy wasn't. It's a movie about injustice, despair, friendship, hope—especially hope—and finally, vindication. In one powerful scene, talking about the sustaining power of music, Andy explained that keeping music alive in the heart demonstrates "there's something inside they can't get to, they can't touch."

"What are you talking about?" Red asks.

"Hope."

> *Hope is to the heart what seeds are to the earth.*

Speaking from a perspective of having spent nearly fifty years in prison, Red says, "Hope is a dangerous thing. It can drive a man insane. It's got no use on the inside of a prison. Better get used to that idea."

But Andy didn't listen. He kept hope alive, and later in the movie, speaking again of the hope of freedom, he sums up the importance of hope with one profound statement, "I guess it comes down to a simple choice, really: get busy livin' or get busy dyin'."

Andy was right. To be without hope is to start the dying process—literally.

In a study reported in the May 2010 issue of *Atherosclerosis*, participants who were persistently depressed had a twofold increased risk of coronary atherosclerosis (narrowing of the arteries). The study took place over a period of ten years, with participants being assessed at least three different times during that ten-year period for depression symptoms.[3] Someone else noted, "This is the same magnitude of increased risk that one sees in comparing a pack-a-day smoker to a nonsmoker."[4]

Incredible. Hopelessness, if not checked, is a death sentence.

A recent study in the *British Medical Journal* confirms this, reporting that people with serious depression were two-thirds more likely to die prematurely; even those with mild depression had a 16 percent higher risk of dying compared to individuals who were distress free.[5] You can die from sorrow!

God told of this a long time ago. Proverbs 13:12 says, "Hope deferred makes the heart sick, but desire fulfilled is a tree of life." Most of you think of your emotional or spiritual heart when you read this, and that is certainly appropriate, but science is now proving that the verse is true of your physical heart as well. Hope deferred creates a diseased heart, both emotionally and physically. And with a diseased heart, no one can run life's race effectively.

"Let us run with endurance the race that is set before us," we are exhorted in Hebrews 12:1. Lack of endurance, however, is one of the first results of heart disease. You may run, but you won't run far. The loss of hope is crippling, making us little more than spectators in life. "Run in such a way that you may win," the Lord urges us through Paul's words in 1 Corinthians 9:24. You'll never do that with a diseased heart. When hope deferred sets in, not only are you unable to win—sometimes you can't even finish the race. Like the suicidal lady in my opening story who had lost the will to live, or Red in *The Shawshank Redemption*, you're too busy dying to live. There's no doubt about it: hope-deferred "heart disease" is a killer.

I don't want the pain, frustration, or disillusionment of hope deferred to affect my heart in any way—and I don't want it to affect yours either. I want you to run the race of life enthusiastically, effectively, and with pleasure, enjoying the journey. You can be certain the Lord wants this for you.

THE COMMON COLD OF THE SOUL

What causes this condition described by the Scriptures as hope deferred? It's really very simple:

unfulfilled or shattered hopes and dreams. For example:

- The death of a loved one

- A failed marriage—or one that never occurred

- A business that went under—you built it and they didn't come

- A family member who still hasn't come to Christ

- An unkept promise

- A gallant fight of faith that was seemingly lost

- Rejection

- Betrayal

- False accusation

- The death of a dream

The list could go on. Regardless of the cause, hope deferred is a common problem that touches everyone. If it now hurts when you think about the dream, you probably have hope deferred. If passion has waned and apathy has encroached, this virus is at work. If you find yourself going through the motions, doing and saying the right things, all the while feeling empty and lifeless on the inside, you may be a victim of this enemy.

If disappointment is stronger than joy in your life, if tears come to your eyes when you think about a certain person, if you can't go to some places in your mind and heart without discomfort or negative emotion, if the promise now sparks disillusionment or cynicism instead of faith, if the statement "God is going to come through for you" is met with doubt or questioning—you're probably experiencing some level of hope-deferred heart disease.

Experiencing this condition doesn't make you bad, weak, or unspiritual. No one makes it through life without suffering some level of this disease. Hope deferred is the common cold of the soul, except that this virus can kill. The symptoms of this illness appear in varying degrees and different forms, ranging from discouragement to depression, doubt to cynicism, and grief to suicidal tendencies. The loss of hope produces resignation, fear, unbelief, loss of passion, retreat from life, and a host of other heart disease maladies.

PRISONER OF HOPE OR HOPELESSNESS

Regardless of which symptoms occur, one thing is certain: the loss of hope imprisons the soul. David, the great worshipper and warrior of Israel, experienced its incarcerating effect while an outcast from Israel. David, though loyal, was being falsely accused of disloyalty to King Saul. He actually had to flee for his life and live in a cave for several years. Look at his prayer, written while he battled the symptoms of hope deferred, in Psalm 142:

> When my spirit was overwhelmed within me, You knew my path. In the way where I walk they have hidden a trap for me. Look to the right and see; for there is no one who regards me; there is no escape for me; no one cares for my soul...." *Bring my soul out of prison,* so that I may give thanks to Your name."
> —PSALM 142:3–4, 7, EMPHASIS ADDED

Hope deferred is the common cold of the soul.

Hope deferred had imprisoned David's soul. Three times in Psalms 42 and 43, also written from the cave, David had to command his soul to hope (Ps. 42:5, 11; 43:5). "Why are you in despair, O my soul? And why have you become disturbed within me? Hope in God, for I shall yet praise Him, the help of my countenance and my God" (Ps. 42:11).

Perhaps life has thrown you a curve, as it did David. The crazy "king" throwing spears at you may be a divorce; your "cave" may be your pain. It doesn't really matter the cause—hope deferred hurts. But don't let this enemy imprison your soul.

Get busy livin'!

God says you can become a "prisoner of hope" (Zech. 9:12, AMP), not of despair. Do as David did—command your soul to hope. He made it out of his prison, and so will you.

In *The Shawshank Redemption* Andy finally tunneled his way out of prison, leaving behind enough evidence to expose the corruption of the cruel warden, and started a new life in Mexico. A short time later Red, who had completely given up on hope, was paroled and joined Andy in his new life, where he too got busy livin' once again.

You may not feel like it now, but you're going to live again. You're going to leave your prison, rise above every disappointment, and reenter life. The power of hope is going to help you: "Now may *the God of hope* fill you with all joy and peace in believing, so that you will *abound in hope* by the power of the Holy Spirit" (Rom. 15:13, emphasis added).

Make plans to live!

REFLECT on the Power of Hope

Have you been struggling with symptoms of hope deferred or heartsickness? What painful experiences came to mind as you read through this chapter? Has your heart been deeply wounded by shattered hopes and dreams—wounds that have yet to heal? Take time to identify the symptoms and sources of hopelessness in your life. Write them on the journal page in the back of this book. Recognizing your areas of need is the first step toward restoration.

APPLY the Power of Hope

James 5:16 encourages us to "confess your sins to one another, and pray for one another so that you may be healed." Identify someone in your life whom you can trust to serve as your accountability and prayer partner throughout your journey to healing. Set up a time to meet this week to share with them your list of symptoms and sources of hopelessness. Even if you can't identify someone who can adequately fill this role in your life, take your list right now and present it to the Lord. Jesus is the greatest friend and prayer partner anyone can have.

PRAY the Power of Hope

Today, Father, I chose to partner with the dreams of Your heart for me—to get busy livin', running the race of life enthusiastically, effectively, and with profound joy. Jesus, I lay down at the foot of Your cross the debilitating burdens of hope deferred that I've carried all this time. I'm trading these ashes in for beauty. No longer will I be a prisoner of hopelessness. I will hope in You, God, and become a vibrant prisoner of hope!

SCRIPTURES TO READ: Proverbs 3:12; Hebrews 12:1; Psalm 42:11; Isaiah 61:1–3; Zechariah 9:12

Chapter Two

YOU WILL CROW AGAIN

A s I said in the last chapter, experiencing the pain of hope deferred doesn't mean you are bad, weak, or unspiritual, and it certainly isn't unusual. It happens to everyone at some point. Consider the following US statistics, all of which are linked to loss of hope. They're not pretty, but they are reality.

- In America there is a divorce every thirteen seconds, which equals 6,646 divorces a day, and 46,523 divorces per week.[1]

- Forty-one percent of first marriages end in divorce, while 60 percent of second marriages and 73 percent of third marriages end in divorce.[2]

- Half of all American children will witness their parents' divorce. Of this number, close to half will witness the breakup of a parent's second marriage.[3]

- Fatherless homes account for 63 percent of youth suicides, 90 percent of homeless/runaway children, and 85 percent of youths in prison.[4]

- Major depressive disorder affects approximately fifteen million American adults in a given year and is the leading cause of disability.[5]

- Suicide is the third leading cause of death among youth between the ages of ten and twenty-four, with approximately forty-six hundred lives lost each year.[6]

- Approximately 14 percent of high school students seriously consider suicide each year, 11 percent have a suicide plan, and 6 percent attempt suicide.[7]

- Twenty-five percent of Americans suffer from mental disorders or substance abuse problems each year.[8]

- Even our spiritual leaders are not immune from this disease—a staggering 70 percent of pastors constantly fight depression.[9]

- Eighty percent of adult children of pastors seek professional help for depression.[10]

- Fifty percent of pastors would leave the ministry if they could but have no other way to make a living.[11]

- Fifteen hundred pastors leave the ministry each month.[12]

CROWNING TOMBS

Whew! Just reading all of that is almost enough to create hope deferred. But here's some great news: hope-deferred heart disease doesn't have to be fatal. There is a fail-proof antidote. Jesus, the great Physician, came "to heal the brokenhearted" (Luke 4:18, KJV), which is obviously an advanced stage of hope deferred. Read the poignant words of Albert Edward Day, slowly and thoughtfully:

> We have confidence that out of the very soil
> that is reddened by the blood of our broken
> hearts, there shall blossom life that is as end-
> less as the life of God. Against all the demons
> of fear and despair that roam through the
> shadows of ignorance and skepticism Jesus
> sets His cross. There it stands today, the
> one sufficient bulwark of our hope, because
> it reveals to us a purpose and a power to
> resolve the tragedy into transfiguration and
> to crown every tomb with the hope of a
> resurrection.[13]

With all of my heart I believe God wants to crown every tomb of your life with a resurrection. Abraham and Sarah discovered this wonderful truth. Theirs was an extreme case of heart disease induced by hope deferred. They laughed cynically when, after twenty-four years of waiting, God came to them one last time promising Isaac. You may even recognize this laugh of cynicism, having experienced it yourself.

> Then Abraham fell on his face and laughed,
> and said in his heart, "Will a child be born
> to a man one hundred years old? And will
> Sarah, who is ninety years old, bear a child?"

And Abraham said to God, "Oh that Ishmael might live before You!"

—GENESIS 17:17–18

He said, "I will surely return to you at this time next year; and behold, Sarah your wife will have a son." And Sarah was listening at the tent door, which was behind him. Now Abraham and Sarah were old, advanced in age; Sarah was past childbearing. Sarah laughed to herself, saying, "After I have become old, shall I have pleasure, my lord being old also?"

—GENESIS 18:10–12

Make no mistake about it; they were in trouble. Once cynicism hits, heart disease is in its advanced stage. Here is a likely progression of unchecked hope deferred:

1. Discouragement—the early stage of this disease

2. Confusion—we begin to question ourselves, our dreams, and God's promises

3. Unbelief—hope is now lost and expectation is gone

4. Disillusionment—which usually involves questioning even the character of God

5. Bitterness—wherein with deep feelings of resentment we blame God, others, and maybe even ourselves

6. Cynicism—a complete loss of faith and hope

In Hope Against Hope

Abraham and Sarah experienced all of the above. Their faith for a child was dead; they were cynical. But their story didn't end there. The God of resurrection stepped in. Listen to His final witness of a restored Abraham and Sarah who broke through into faith and fulfillment, just as you are going to do.

> In hope against hope he believed, so that he might become a father of many nations according to that which had been spoken, "So shall your descendants be."
> —Romans 4:18

> By faith even Sarah herself received ability to conceive, even beyond the proper time of life, since she considered Him faithful who had promised.
> —Hebrews 11:11

If Abraham and Sarah could move from such an extreme stage of hope deferred to strong, vibrant faith, you can as well. "In hope against hope" is a powerful phrase. It means that in the face of absolute hopelessness, Abraham hoped anyway.

Then there was Moses, the heart-diseased cynic who refused to believe God could ever use him again. Who can blame him? After all, forty years of failure and isolation is a lot of hope deferred! Consider his response to God's commission to lead Israel out of Egypt. "Who am I, that I should go to Pharaoh, and that I should bring the sons of Israel out of Egypt?" (Exod. 3:11).

The account in Exodus chapters 3 and 4 makes it clear that Moses had completely run out of hope. His tank was empty, and he was past believing. Any faith he had for fulfilling his destiny and helping his fellow Israelites had been dead for a long time. But the God who brings hope to the hopeless reentered his life through a burning bush, opened up his clogged arteries, gave him a good shot of adrenaline, and said, "Let's go, Moses. I'm not finished with you." I'll say! Listen to Moses's victorious epitaph:

> Since that time no prophet has risen in Israel like Moses, whom the LORD knew face to face, for all the signs and wonders which the LORD sent him to perform in the land of

Egypt against Pharaoh, all his servants, and all his land, and for all the mighty power and for all the great terror which Moses performed in the sight of all Israel.

—DEUTERONOMY 34:10–12

That qualifies as a bona fide overcomer of hope deferred!

THE BEGINNING OF A NEW DAY

Craig Brian Larson relates a story told in the *Pentecostal Evangel* by J. K. Gressett, who wrote about a man named Samuel S. Scull, who settled in the Arizona desert with his family:

One night a fierce desert storm struck with rain, hail, and a high wind. At daybreak, feeling sick and fearing what he might find, Samuel went to survey their loss.

The hail had beaten the garden into the ground; the house was partially unroofed; the henhouse had blown away and dead chickens were scattered about. Destruction and devastation were everywhere.

While standing dazed, evaluating the mess and wondering about the future, he heard a stirring in the lumber pile that was the remains of the henhouse. A rooster was climbing up, and continued until he had mounted the highest board in the pile. That old rooster was dripping wet, and most of his feathers were blown away. But as the sun came over the eastern horizon, he flapped his bony wings and proudly crowed.[14]

When the morning sun appeared on the horizon, that beat-up, featherless rooster—amidst all the chaos and devastation—still crowed, announcing the beginning of a new day. Why? *Because it was his nature to do so.*

Winds of adversity may have blown through your life. Your world may be falling apart. But if you will look closely enough, you'll see the light of God's faithfulness shining through the debris. And you can rise above the devastation *because it is your nature to overcome!* Listen to what God says about you in Romans 8:35–39. It is laced with the power of hope.

Do you think anyone is going to be able to drive a wedge between us and Christ's love for us? There is no way! Not trouble, not hard times, not hatred, not hunger, not homelessness, not bullying threats, not backstabbing, not even the worst sins listed in Scripture....None of this fazes us because Jesus loves us. I'm absolutely convinced that nothing—nothing living or dead, angelic or demonic, today or tomorrow, high or low, thinkable or unthinkable—absolutely *nothing* can get between us and God's love because of the way that Jesus our Master has embraced us.

—THE MESSAGE

Your world may be falling apart. But if you will look closely enough, you'll see the light of God's faithfulness shining through the debris.

Before God is finished, you're going to climb up out of the debris, flap your bony wings, and announce to the world that you've entered a new day. Why? Because deep in your DNA you're an overcomer! God programmed you to heal, to overcome, and to win.

Like Abraham you will believe, like Sarah you will conceive, and like Moses you will rise from your isolation and exile. You will live again. God is determined to reverse your tragedy into transformation and crown your tomb with the testimony of a glorious resurrection.

From there, your own empty tomb, you will crow.

———•◦•———

REFLECT on the Power of Hope

Review the list of six progressive symptoms of unchecked hope deferred to determine the extent of your heartsickness. Now take time to reflect upon these words: God wants to turn your tragedy into transfiguration and crown every tomb of your life with the testimony of a glorious resurrection.

APPLY the Power of Hope

Think of ways in which you've seen the light of God's faithfulness shine through the darkest nights of your soul. On the journal page in the back of this book, write down the memories that come to mind. What could happen if you were to engage with the Lord's promptings and "hope against hope"? Take more notes as you dream.

PRAY the Power of Hope

I thank You, God of hope, for Your desire to fully heal and restore life to my diseased, broken heart. As I look back over my life, I am grateful for each time You reentered my hopeless state and met me in that dark place of despair. Thank You for pursuing me with Your relentless love and never giving up on me. Your love has made it possible for me to hope against hope and find real hope once again. My life will be beautifully transformed and crowned with the testimony of a glorious resurrection.

SCRIPTURES TO READ: Romans 15:13; Luke 4:18; Romans 4:18, 8:35–39; 2 Corinthians 3:18; Isaiah 61:1–3

Chapter Three

FACE THE WIND

Y WIFE, CECI, and I have lived in Colorado for twenty years. We love the state, with all of its majestic mountains, amazing wildlife, and beautiful streams. Tough guy that I am, one of the first things I decided to do when we moved there was take up running—not just any running, mind you, but running on some beautiful mountainous hills. Exhilarating.

"You might want to wait a few weeks," one of my friends advised, "until your body acclimates to the altitude. For the first few weeks you'll be subject to shortness of breath. Eventually your body will create more red blood cells, which will carry more oxygen to your body."

Giving him my what-kind-of-a-wimp-are-you look, I smugly and arrogantly replied, "I'm an athlete and I'm fit! I will not get tired or lose my breath."

Have you ever seen a man beside a mountain trail in an absolute state of spasmodic panic, flailing his arms, bending over, beating his chest, and gasping for breath? If so, it may have been me! When this suffocating experience hits, it's traumatic. It's like sucking air and holding your breath at the same time! It's weird, confusing, and scary. And it'll make you stop running—*you will stop running!*

Just like hope deferred.

One of the first symptoms of heart disease—the end result of unresolved hope deferred—is shortness of breath. And I guarantee you, you won't run. Walk? Perhaps. Run? No way. You'll lose the *strength*, and the *will*, to run life's race. A weak heart simply can't sustain you on the mountainous terrain of life.

HEART DISEASE PHASE #1: LOSS OF FAITH

I want to point out four debilitating results of losing hope and, therefore, losing heart. The first of them is *a loss of faith in God's goodness and provision.* There are many wonderful Christians who are still able to maintain their Christian *lifestyle* but are unable to maintain strong *faith.* They're alive but anemic.

The Bible speaks of having a *form* of godliness

while denying the *power* thereof (2 Tim. 3:5). Many Christians go through the motions, demonstrating the form or lifestyle of Christianity, while having lost the reality of the experience. They walk out their Christianity, as far as its outward expression is concerned, yet experience very little, if any, internal joy, peace, faith, or fire.

Jesus said of the church at Sardis in Revelation 3:1–2: "You have a name that you are alive, but you are dead. Wake up, and strengthen the things that remain, which were about to die; for I have not found your deeds completed in the sight of My God." Though their condition was caused by complacency and compromise, not hope deferred, nonetheless they depict the potential of a believer to experience form without substance.

I find it interesting that this church's reputation was still intact. In other words, among the rest of the body of Christ, their reputation was still that they were a church filled with passion, perhaps even on fire. You can often fool others with your outward expression, but you can't fool God. Jesus was able to look into their hearts and discern that though they were doing all the right things, demonstrating the right forms, and going through the proper routines, inside they were dying. How tragic—and how common.

Zacharias, John the Baptist's father, was a victim of hope deferred. He was a priest in the temple and was "righteous...walking blamelessly in all the commandments and requirements of the Lord" (Luke 1:6). Not bad! Yet when an angel appeared to him as he performed the incense offering, informing him that he and Elizabeth would have a son, he simply couldn't believe it. Why? Hope deferred had stolen his faith. While still able to religiously serve, his faith was too weak to receive. "Impossible," he thought. "Two people our age having a child? I don't think so." Elizabeth had been a barren woman, and now they were old. Hopelessness had set in, and Zacharias could not respond in faith, not even to an angelic visitation. His hope-deferred past outweighed this hope-filled promise, even from an angel.

How often we are like Zacharias! We go to the "temple"—our church services—every week, "performing" our Christian duties. Like Zacharias we worship, presenting our version of an incense offering to God. But many of us, if we're honest, will admit that we have areas in our hearts where hope deferred has robbed us of our ability to believe for anything truly supernatural. We have form, but we have lost the power.

Please don't feel condemned. There probably is not a Christian alive who hasn't experienced this to one degree or another. We're like the lame man at the pool of Bethesda, who, after many years of waiting for a miracle, had lost all hope. (See John 5:7.) Jesus first had to bring him back to a place of hope. "Do you still want to get well?" He asked him.

When hope deferred poisons the heart, you still show up, but there's really no faith that you'll receive. You lay hands on the sick but don't really expect them to recover. You pray for revival but question if it will actually come. You lift your hands in worship on Sunday morning, but your heart is cold and you think little about the things of God the rest of the week.

> *Many of us, if we're honest, will admit that we have areas in our hearts where hope deferred has robbed us of our ability to believe for anything truly supernatural.*

Plainly stated, hope deferred, if it doesn't cause you to turn away from God, has the potential to make you nothing more than "religious" in your dealings and relationship with Him. It is Christianity dressed in religious clothing—forms, routines, and actions— yet faithless and out of breath.

If you find yourself in this condition, don't yield to the condemnation, and don't give up. This is a book about *overcoming* hope deferred, not being *ashamed* of it. There is always a way to victory in God. Before you finish this book, your heart will be on its way to recovery. Persevere! You are an overcomer in the deepest part of your spiritual DNA, "for everyone born of God overcomes the world. This is the victory that has overcome the world, even our faith" (1 John 5:4, NIV).

HEART DISEASE PHASE #2: LOSS OF COURAGE

A cousin to the loss of vibrant faith in God is *a loss of courage*. These are often two symptoms of the same disease. Nothing erodes courage like the loss of hope. It clogs spiritual arteries like an overdose of cholesterol, and, if this loss is left unchecked, a heart attack is in the future.

One of my favorite stories in the Bible is of David and Goliath. I love the part when David, after boldly declaring that God would give Goliath into his hands, "ran quickly toward the battle line to meet the Philistine" (1 Sam. 17:48). That's what I call running with a courageous heart. On another occasion David said, "I pursued my enemies and overtook them, and I did not turn back until they were consumed" (Ps. 18:37).

Your heritage as a believer in the Lord is to be like David, bold as a lion and on the offensive. Scripture teaches that your enemies should flee from you, not the other way around. (See Deuteronomy 28:7; Proverbs 28:1.)

I'm referring to spiritual and emotional enemies, of course, not other human beings. You should always seek to avoid physical confrontations, if at all possible. On other occasions you may have to escape from oppressive or abusive situations. These scenarios you may flee *from*; spiritual and emotional enemies you should boldly run *toward*.

Hope deferred, however, produces fear and makes you uncertain of yourself and, yes, even of your God. When you should be able to move forward in faith, believing you are more than a conqueror, you find yourself operating in fear and timidity, fleeing from the adversities and giants of your life.

Hebrews 12:12 warns of this: "Strengthen...the knees that are feeble," it admonishes us. "Feeble" is translated from the Greek word *paraluo*, from which we derive our English word "paralyzed." It's true, isn't it? Fear paralyzes. You've probably heard the phrase "frozen with fear" or "petrified" as descriptions of the paralyzing power of fear. It immobilizes you. Other translations of this verse picture well the connection between *paraluo* and fear: strengthen "your shaky knees," one version reads; another says, "stand firm on your shaky legs"; and still another, "stiffen the stand on your knocking knees."[1] None of them are very edifying.

Israel's behavior when facing the giants controlling their promised inheritance is a classic example of the paralysis caused by hopelessness. After experiencing a glorious deliverance from Egypt, in which God totally emaciated their enemies and showed Himself strong at every point, the Israelites found themselves hopelessly intimidated when facing the giants of Canaan. Initially they expected God to deal with the Canaanites in the same way He had with the Egyptians. When that didn't occur, hope deferred began its paralyzing work, fear began to grow, and there was a great erosion of confidence in the hearts of the Israelites.

The next step was predictable, and Israel did what many do, magnifying their enemies' power above even God's.

Hope deferred distorts your vision. Looking at your enemies through the lens of hope deferred is like looking at them through a magnifying glass. "We became like grasshoppers in our own sight," the Israeli spies said (Num. 13:33).

Overreaction is usually next. Mark Twain once said, "I am an old man and have known a great many troubles, but most of them have never happened."[2] How true! When fear sets in, rather than *act* in confidence to life's challenges, we *overreact*, pushing the adrenaline of panic into our hearts. Listen to the sound of hope deferred-induced heart failure:

> Then all the congregation lifted up their voices and cried, and the people wept that night. All the sons of Israel grumbled against Moses and Aaron; and the whole congregation said to them, "Would that we had died in the land of Egypt! Or would that we had died in this wilderness! Why is the LORD bringing us into this land, to fall by the sword? Our wives and our little ones will become plunder; would it not be better for us to return to Egypt?" So they said to one another, "Let us appoint a leader and return to Egypt."
>
> —NUMBERS 14:1–4

Looking at your enemies through the lens of hope deferred is like looking at them through a magnifying glass.

You can probably relate. I can. I'm appalled at how quickly I have gone from the mountaintop of victory and faith to the valley of deep despair. When this occurs, rather than receiving strategy from the Lord and boldly taking action, I find myself inwardly cowering in the face of adversity. If this process isn't stopped early, the giants grow larger while my faith becomes smaller. Eventually slavery in Egypt can be more appealing than conquering the giants controlling my future! This is exactly what occurred with that generation of Israelites.

REFUSE TO BECOME A VICTIM

Refuse to become a hopeless victim. God wants to heal your heart, fill you with the power of hope, and cause you to be bold in Him. Hope-killing giants look small when measured against Him.

Be like President John F. Kennedy during his show-down with Russia in 1962: "Khrushchev reminds me of the tiger hunter who has picked a place on the wall to hang the tiger skin long before he has caught the tiger. This tiger has other ideas."[3] When life's "hunters" come looking for your hope and courage, resist them immediately. Tell them you have other ideas!

Thomas Edison refused to become a victim. Listen to his amazing refusal to lose hope.

> In December 1914, a great, sweeping fire destroyed Thomas Edison's laboratories in West Orange, New Jersey, wiping out two million dollars' worth of equipment and the record of much of his life's work.
>
> Edison's son Charles ran about frantically

trying to find his father. Finally he came upon him, standing near the fire, his face ruddy in the glow, his white hair blown by the winter winds. "My heart ached for him," Charles Edison said. "He was no longer young and everything was being destroyed. He spotted me. 'Where's your mother?' he shouted. 'Find her. Bring her here. She'll never see anything like this again as long as she lives.'"

The next morning, walking about the charred embers of so many of his hopes and dreams, the sixty-seven-year-old Edison said, "There is great value in disaster. All our mistakes are burned up. Thank God we can start anew."[4]

You can't beat a man or a woman with hope that strong. No way. To them, God will always be bigger than their giants. The prophet Jeremiah, looking at the smoldering ruins of Jerusalem, said much the same thing. Though he lamented, he did so with hope:

> This I recall to my mind, therefore I have hope. Through the LORD's mercies we are not consumed, because His compassions fail not. They are new every morning; great is

Your faithfulness. "The LORD is my portion,"
says my soul, "therefore I hope in Him!"
—LAMENTATIONS 3:21–24, NKJV

Responses such as these seem contrary to human sanity—and indeed they are! But they reveal the paradoxical nature of an irrepressible hope in God—a hoping against hope, a joy unspeakable, and a peace that passes understanding (Rom. 4:18; Phil 4:7; 1 Pet. 1:8).

Have the attitude of the small bird in the midst of a storm that "was clinging to the limb of a tree, seemingly calm and unafraid. As the wind tore at the limbs of the tree, the bird continued to look the storm in the face, as if to say, 'Shake me off; I still have wings.'"[5]

Face the adverse wind—you have wings!

REFLECT on the Power of Hope

Think of ways in which you have seen the first two results of losing hope and heart at work in your life. Write down your thoughts in the journal section of this book.

- Loss of faith in God's goodness and provision
- Loss of courage—paralyzed by fear, distorted vision, overreaction

APPLY the Power of Hope

Review your responses concerning each of the areas outlined in the REFLECT section. With a determination to boldly run toward, pursue, and overtake these enemies of your heart, write out a statement that asserts the opposite of each manifestation of hopeless heartsickness. Bible scriptures can provide some great guidance for developing these statements. For example, regarding overreaction, one can say: "I will be anxious for nothing, but in everything by prayer and supplication with thanksgiving I will let my requests be made known to God" (Phil. 4:6).

PRAY the Power of Hope

Discerner of hearts, I thank You for awakening me to my condition and setting me on a journey to strengthen what remains.

Today I can believe for breakthrough, and I choose to run to the battle line, armed with Your hope-filled promises. I will trust in Your goodness, move forward in faith, focus upon Your greatness, and still my heart to rest in You. For in You, Jesus, I will have victory over my enemies.

SCRIPTURES TO READ: Romans 3:1–2; Hebrews 12:12; 1 Samuel 17:48; Psalm 18:37; 1 John 5:4; Lamentations 3:21–24

Chapter Four

LAUGHTER IS COMING

IN THE LAST chapter we looked at two phases of the heart disease caused by hopelessness. The first was a loss of faith in God's goodness and provision; the second was a loss of courage. When these two things are happening, you may not yet be in cardiac arrest, but you're well on your way.

HEART DISEASE PHASE #3: LOSS OF OUR GOD CONNECTION

Failed expectations can be so devastating and debilitating! Like a balloon that has lost its air, the rapid deflation of your heart sends your emotions haphazardly spinning out of control. If you're not careful, the next step in the heart disease process *is a loss of our God connection.* When this happens, the flow of life stops; a complete blockage has occurred.

This is what took place with Christ's disciples. Not expecting things to turn out as they had—the devastation of the cross, the ecstasy of the resurrection, and then Christ's complete disappearance—these guys' emotions had reached their limits. Who can blame them? So, in frustration and confusion they began to disconnect, making plans to return to their old lives and vocations: "I am going fishing," their leader Peter declared (John 21:3).

The other hope-depleted disciples said, in essence, "We're with you, Peter. Enough of this confusing 'save the world' stuff; enough of crosses, resurrections, and ascensions. It was fun for a while. But this is all a little too confusing for us. Fishing? That we understand! Let's go."

Please understand that the disciples were not fishing simply to take a break. They were running from what they couldn't understand and returning to what they could: their former occupation.

Surely you've been there. Hopelessness and despair disoriented you; then you lost your bearings, your focus. And then perhaps, like the disciples, you retreated. But like the disciples, you don't always realize that sometimes when you run from the confusion, you're running from your purpose and destiny.

I love Christ's response to the disciples' confusion and hopelessness. Scripture says, "That night they caught nothing" (John 21:3). It's a real bummer to fish all night and catch nothing. But think about it—do you really believe that result was simply bad luck? No way!

In His love and commitment to them, Jesus was arresting their retreat. "I love you too much to let you prosper in your confused retreat," He was telling them. "I won't allow you to succeed in going back to your old life." Christ was much too committed to their destiny and His mission to allow that to occur.

Christ then worked one of His now familiar miracles, telling them to throw their net out on the other side of the boat, which resulted in a great catch. Then He prepared them a meal right there on the beach, spent some time interacting with them, and recommissioned them to their calling. His intervention stopped the heart attack, removing the blockages and opening the flow. What did His actions communicate to them and to us?

- "Even when you don't understand, I want you to trust Me."

- "Even though you no longer see Me all the time, I'm still around. Do not fear."

- "I told you I would make you fishers of
  men, and I'm jealously guarding that
  destiny. Now, rekindle your hope and
  get back to the race I have for you." (See
  John 21:15–17.)

- "Hope deferred isn't terminal, guys.
  Hang in there—you'll understand
  shortly. Until then, trust Me."

You and I must trust Him also. When plans seem to have changed and He didn't inform you, trust Him. Don't disconnect. When things don't seem to make sense, He's somewhere near, preparing you a meal that will sustain you until your breakthrough. Trust Him.

Hebrews 6:18–19 (emphasis added) tells you what your response should be when disappointment and confusion come.

> *We who have taken refuge would have strong*
> *encouragement to take hold of the hope set*
> *before us.* This hope we have as an anchor of
> the soul, a hope both sure and steadfast and
> one which enters within the veil.

Anchor yourself to Him!

I love the great hymn "My Hope Is Built." It so eloquently states what our response to adversity should be: "My hope is built on nothing less than Jesus' blood and righteousness." I especially love the following verses:

> When darkness seems to hide His face,
> I rest on His unchanging grace.
> In every high and stormy gale,
> My anchor holds within the veil.
>
> His oath, His covenant, His blood,
> Support me in the whelming flood.
> When all around my soul gives way,
> He then is all my Hope and Stay.[1]

He is your hope. Anchor yourself to Him. In every storm, in every flood, stay anchored.

HEART DISEASE PHASE #4: CYNICISM TOWARD GOD'S PROMISES

The last phase of hope-deferred heart disease is *a complete cynicism toward God's promises.* You may be surprised by my first and primary example: Abraham and Sarah, the founders of the Jewish race and givers of the Messiah. I mentioned them in chapter 2, but let's take a closer look.

After ten years of waiting for Isaac, Abraham and Sarah succumbed to the relentless barrage of hopelessness. I completely understand. Ten years is a long time to wait for a promise, especially when the promise is that you will have your dreamed-of child. With Sarah having been barren all of her life, and both of them growing older, hope was gone. The result was Ishmael, a child through Sarah's maid, and along with him a divided family and centuries of conflict. Running ahead of God creates major problems.

Abraham and Sarah then did what many of us do: they asked God to accept their connived, compromising solution and do things their way. "Oh that Ishmael might live before You!" Abraham cried out (Gen. 17:18). In other words, let him be the promised child.

How pathetically human! "I was tired of waiting for Your plan to unfold, God, so I came up with one of my own. Now, please let mine become Yours." Too often our actions demonstrate this very mindset. How many times have I grown impatient when waiting for God's plan to unfold and decided to generate one of my own? Too many.

God, however, is convinced that His way is always best and that His time is always right. He refuses to accept the Ishmaels born of your hopeless, diseased heart. You are intimidated by the supernatural element needed to fulfill God's purpose for you; He, of course, is not. God wants you dependent on Him and therefore gives you a destiny that rises above anything you could possibly produce on your own.

This isn't unkind on His part; it is gracious and glorious. Who would want to settle for a natural inheritance when they can have a supernatural one? It's easy, of course, to pontificate these theologically sound and lofty ideals when you're not the one waiting for an Isaac!

God actually waited another thirteen years before bringing Isaac. By then, both Abraham and Sarah no longer even entertained the idea of a son. Why would they? Abraham was ninety-eight, and Sarah was eighty-nine! But God appeared to them and said, "At this time next year you will have a son."

> *God wants you dependent on Him and therefore gives you a destiny that rises above anything you could possibly produce on your own.*

I don't know about you, but I know what I would have done—the exact thing both Abraham and Sarah did. They laughed. And not a laugh of joy, mind you, but of cynicism. God was neither offended by their laughter nor intimidated by their ages. He isn't cocky, but He is very confident. He thinks He can do anything!

But sure enough, a year later Isaac was born. And God, with His great sense of humor, insisted on the name Isaac, which means "laughter." Do you think He was mocking Abraham and Sarah's cynical laugh? I don't. I believe it was God's forever reminder that He can always heal your hope-deferred heart disease, even when you're in complete cardiac arrest, and completely resurrect your faith. "Walk with Me," He says, "and your laugh of cynicism will become the satisfying laugh of newborn parents."

New Life to Dead Hopes

When we do run ahead of God and produce an Ishmael—and who hasn't?—God will remove him. Ishmael will have to go. (See Genesis 21:9–14.) This can be painful, but we can also rejoice in the fact that "when we have spoiled His plan for us by our folly or ignorance, He has another waiting. Every day is a fresh beginning, and the future is radiant with another chance. His imperial voice will bid the dead hopes of yesterday to rise in newness of life and fill the later days with glorious achievement."[2]

Dead hopes of yesterday rising in newness of life. That would be Isaac! George Frideric Handel, composer of the great oratorio *Messiah*, demonstrated that wonderful truth.

He was a has-been, a fossil, a relic, an old fogy...but it hadn't always been so. As a child, George Frideric Handel had accompanied his father to the court of Duke Johann Adolf....By his twenties he was the talk of England and the best paid composer on earth....

But the glory passed. Audiences dwindled. His music became outdated....One project after another failed, and Handel grew depressed. The stress brought on a case of palsy that crippled some of his fingers. "Handel's great days are over," wrote Frederick the Great, "his inspiration is exhausted."

Yet his troubles also matured him...and his music became more heartfelt. One morning Handel received by post a script from Charles Jennens. It was a word-for word collection of various biblical texts about Christ. The opening words from Isaiah 40 moved Handel: *Comfort ye my people.*

On August 22, 1741, he...started composing music for the words. Twenty-three days later, the world had *Messiah*....*Messiah* opened in London to enormous crowds on March 23, 1743. Handel led from his harpsichord, and King George II, who was present that night, surprised everyone by leaping to his feet during *Hallelujah Chorus*...from that day audiences everywhere have stood in reverence during the stirring words: *Hallelujah! For He shall reign forever and ever.*[3]

Aren't you glad Handel allowed God to rid him of his Ishmaels and bring Isaac to us? Millions have been stirred by its majestic cadence and powerful declaration. There's an Isaac in you also. A fresh start. And like Abraham and Sarah you will laugh—not the cynical laugh of hope deferred, but the joyous laugh of fulfilled expectations.

REFLECT on the Power of Hope

This chapter describes two additional phases in the progression toward heart disease caused by hopelessness. Think of ways in which you have seen these symptoms of advanced heartsickness at work in your life. Write down your thoughts in the journal section of this book.

- A loss of our God connection—running from God and to what's familiar
- Complete cynicism toward God's promises

APPLY the Power of Hope

Review your responses concerning the two areas outlined in the REFLECT section. Laying hold of the conviction that God has the power to make all things new and completely resurrect a heart in cardiac arrest, use the journal section to write out statements that assert the opposite of these last two manifestations of hopeless heartsickness. Read your statements aloud, and in response, release the laughter of life-giving victory within!

PRAY the Power of Hope

Father, I thank You for loving me too much to allow me to prosper in running away from You and back to my old ways. I repent for having yielded to the confusion and adversity and for producing Ishmaels out of my sick, hopeless heart. I am grateful for being given a supernatural destiny and inheritance that rise above anything I can possibly produce on my own. Jesus, I choose to trust You, run to You, and lay hold of the hope You've set before me. Despite dead hopes and a diseased heart, my future is radiant, for You make all things new.

SCRIPTURES TO READ: John 21:15–17; Hebrews 6:18–19; Jeremiah 29:11; Psalm 31:3; Revelation 21:5

Chapter Five

THERE IS MUSIC IN YOU STILL

T HE STORY IS told in *Chicken Soup for the Unsinkable Soul*, "It was a chilly fall day when the farmer spied a little sparrow lying on its back in the middle of his field. The farmer stopped his plowing, looked down at the frail, feathered creature, and inquired, 'Why are you lying upside down like that?'

"'I heard the sky is going to fall today,' replied the bird.

"The old farmer chuckled, 'And I suppose your spindly little legs can hold up the sky?'

"'One does what one can,' replied the plucky sparrow."[1]

I'm always amazed at how God uses spindly little

humans to get things accomplished. The apostle Paul understood this. He said that God's "strength is made perfect in weakness" (2 Cor. 12:9, KJV). Gideon understood it too. He and 300 soldiers faced an army of 135,000, using torches and pitchers as weapons. (See Judges 6–8.) I'd call that a spindly little army. It reminds me of the phrase we've already mentioned from Romans 4:18 to describe Abraham: "In hope against hope he believed."

If I understand that phrase correctly, it means that when there was absolutely no hope, Abraham hoped anyway. Spiros Zodhiates says it means "in spite of" or "without ground of hope."[2] With no grounds for hope, in spite of the impossibility of the situation, Abraham hoped anyway. This concept is like the "but God" phrases in Scripture. There are many; here are a couple:

> And as for you, you meant evil against me [Joseph], *but God* meant it for good in order to bring about this present result, to preserve many people alive.
> —GENESIS 50:20, EMPHASIS ADDED

> "And now shall I [Samson] die of thirst and fall into the hands of the uncircumcised?" *But God* split the hollow place that is in Lehi

so that water came out of it. When he drank,
his strength returned and he revived.
—JUDGES 15:18–19, EMPHASIS ADDED

The point is that at times no human hope or ability
exists in a particular situation, *but God* shows up!
That's what He wants to do in your life—enter your
hopeless scenario and invade your hope-deferred
world. In this chapter we begin to facilitate that powerful process. Like Abraham, begin to hope against
all hope. After all, that's what faith is—believing in
something you can't yet see or feel.

MUSIC IN YOUR SOUL

One night a discouraged man in London was on his
way to drown himself. At that moment his life did not
seem worth living. As he walked along the street, he
stopped and looked at a painting in a shop window. It
was George Frederic Watt's *Hope*—a woman, blind-
folded, sitting on top of the world, holding a lyre
with but one string. Yet still hoping and believing the
instrument will make music, she is ready to strike it.
The man, as he stood looking at that painting, said to
himself: "Well, I have one string—I have a little boy
at home." So he returned home to his son.[3]

When you feel you have nothing left, look again.
The prophet Habakkuk said the flock might be dead
and gone, there might be no fruit in the orchard, and

the hillsides might be bare. But still, "I will exult in the Lord," he said. "I will rejoice in the God of my salvation." (See Habakkuk 3:17–19.) There was music possible yet!

And there is music left in you. I know you can play hope's song, even in the dark night of the soul. Job, in his hellish suffering, said the Lord "gives songs in the night" (Job 35:10). David, during his time of exile, said, "His song will be with me in the night" (Ps. 42:8). Paul and Silas, beaten, bleeding and in chains, "about midnight...were praying and singing hymns of praise to God" (Acts 16:25). There is hope in the night, and there is music somewhere in your soul. Don't give up!

GIDEON MEETS THE LORD OUR WHOLENESS

As I mentioned, Gideon had a spindly little army. To make matters worse, he had contracted a pretty severe case of hope deferred. In Gideon's day Israel, because of their idolatry, was being severely oppressed by the Midianites. Sometimes you're responsible for the hope deferred in your life; sometimes you're a victim. This situation had clearly been created by the Israelites themselves. God, however, is a God of great mercy, and He was about to forgive their sin and bring deliverance.

As He often does, God chose as His instrument a

person who appeared to be very unqualified for the task. At this point in his life Gideon certainly wasn't a man of great faith or hope. In fact, when the Lord called him a valiant warrior and said He was with him, Gideon's hope deferred became very obvious; his response was filled with unbelief and cynicism.

> Then Gideon said to him, "O my lord, *if* the Lord is with us, *why* then has all this happened to us? And *where* are all His miracles which our fathers told us about, saying, 'Did not the Lord bring us up from Egypt?' But now *the Lord has abandoned us* and given us into the hand of Midian."
> —JUDGES 6:13, EMPHASIS ADDED

Gideon's, and all of Israel's, heartsick, hope-deferred condition had progressed to the point where, for the most part, they did not expect God to come through for them. All of their faith and devotion had been transferred to the false gods of Baal and Asherah. We often do the same thing, though often in a more subtle way. We may not set up literal idols as Israel did, but we do sometimes waver in our devotion to God and place our trust in other things: ourselves, other people, money, government, drugs, alcohol, pleasures, success, and perhaps even other religions.

Notice, however, the kind and forgiving response of the Lord to this condition that plagued Gideon and the Israelites. He was about to reveal Himself to them in a new way: as the God who heals hope deferred. Gideon had decided to offer a sacrifice to his heavenly visitor, and while he was doing so, fire sprang up from the rock on which he had laid the sacrifice and consumed the offering. Gideon, of course, was terrified by this awesome display of power. Knowing this, the messenger said something very important to him, "Peace [*Shalom*] to you" (Judg. 6:23).

> We may not set up literal idols as Israel did, but we do sometimes waver in our devotion to God and place our trust in other things.

Most of us have a very limited understanding of this word translated "peace." While it does indeed mean tranquility or calmness, the word carries far more meaning than that. The basic concept contained in this word is *wholeness*. As Zodhiates says, "It is a sense of well-being...to be unharmed or unhurt...it expressed completeness, harmony, and fulfillment."[4]

What the angel of the Lord, whom many scholars believe was an Old Testament appearance of Jesus, literally said to Gideon was, "Wholeness to you,

Gideon." While the Lord may have been attempting to alleviate Gideon's temporary fear of Him, He was also ministering healing and wholeness to him in an overall sense. Gideon was so moved by the experience that he built an altar to the Lord and called it Jehovah Shalom, which became one of the popular redemption names of the Lord. The name means, "the Lord our wholeness." That would not have been done to commemorate a simple word bringing comfort only for a brief moment.

GOD WANTS TO INVADE YOUR HOPE-DEFERRED WORLD

The Lord was breaking hope deferred off of Gideon. His holy and awesome presence was healing him. God wants to visit you in your troubled state and do the same for you. He wants to invade your insecure world of pain, despair, and disillusionment; bring fire from His altar; and speak a word of wholeness to you. The word may come through a sermon, a friend, scripture, or the quiet voice of the Lord in your heart, but of this you can be certain: God has a healing word for you.

For Sherry, in the following story, Jehovah Shalom came in a most unusual way.

Sherry was visiting another city when she noticed a gloriously beautiful sunset. Wanting to share it with someone, she asked a clerk in the nearby store to come outside. Obviously puzzled, the woman followed her outside.

"Just look at that sunset!" Sherry said. "God's in His heaven and all's right with the world." After briefly enjoying the beauty, the clerk went back inside and Sherry left.

Four years later, Sherry was recently divorced, on her own for the first time, living in reduced circumstances, and feeling very discouraged. She came across a magazine article about a woman who had been in similar circumstances. This woman had come to the end of a marriage, moved to strange community, worked at a job she didn't like, and was struggling. Then something profound happened. A woman came into her store and asked her to step outside. The stranger pointed to the sunset and said, "God's in His heaven and all's right with the world." Realizing the truth in that statement, the clerk turned her life around.

Sherry's perspective changed too, after reading the article—the gift of hope had come full circle.[5]

Sherry's healing word did, indeed, come in a most unusual way, and through an even more surprising vessel—herself. God knows what you need to hear and when you need to hear it. Keep listening. Just as He spoke to Gideon, Sherry, and thousands of others, He will speak to you.

CHOOSING HOPE AND HEALING

At this point in Gideon's story, when the offer of wholeness came, he faced a decision. Gideon could have stopped the process right there, saying, "I'm not ready for this." He could have allowed his past frustrations, pains, fears, and diseased heart to keep him from progressing toward hope. This was a crisis point, one we all reach, in the process of healing from hope deferred: choosing to embrace the healing process.

Hope—and healing—is a choice that must be made.

As you probably know too well, experiencing hope deferred does not require a choice—pain and disappointment are facts of life. Healing, however, does. Making the simple but powerful choice to hope again is the first step toward healing.

Wilma Rudolph, three-time gold medalist in the 1960 Olympics and once known in the field of running as the world's fastest woman, said, "The doctors told me I would never walk again. My mother told me I would. I believed my mother."[6]

Born prematurely into a very poor family, and the twentieth of twenty-two children, Wilma was not permitted to receive care at the local white hospital. For the next several years her mother nursed her through her illnesses. When Wilma contracted polio, her mother took her once a week for two years to the nearest medical facility that would treat her—a ninety-mile round trip. Wilma Rudolph's life is an amazing story of achievement against the odds; but the story began with right choices.[7]

Like the Olympic champion and her mother, you will have to choose the power of hope. I realize this puts some of the responsibility for healing on you, but it is also an incredibly liberating truth. Healing—freedom from hope deferred—is a choice that *can* be made. Scripture is filled with promises that you have this power to choose life over death. The Lord actually told the Israelites to "choose life" (Deut. 30:19). You don't have the luxury of choosing never to have challenges, but you do get to choose how you respond. The following story pictures this well.

William Carey, the "Father of Modern Missions," wanted to translate the Bible into as many Indian languages as possible. Early in 1832, his associate discovered flames engulfing their printing room. Although workers fought the blaze, everything was destroyed.

The next day, another missionary traveled to Carey's location. "I can think of no easy way to break this news," he said. "The print shop burned to the ground last night."

Carey was stunned. His complete library was gone, including dictionaries, grammar books and Bibles, as well as typesets for fourteen languages. "The work of years—gone in a moment," he whispered.

Carey took little time to mourn. "The loss is heavy," he wrote, "but we are not discouraged; indeed the work is already begun again in every language. *We are cast down but not in despair.*"

News of the fire catapulted Carey to instant fame in England. Funds were raised and volunteers offered to help. By the end of that year, portions of Scripture, even entire Bibles, had been issued in forty-four languages and dialects.

The secret of Carey's success was his resiliency. "There are grave difficulties on every hand" he once wrote, "and more are looming ahead. But we must go forward."[8]

William Carey made the right choice. He stared adversity and lack in the face, declaring, "There is a song in this night." You can do the same. Don't wait another moment. Do it *now*! You don't have to be well to hope, but you do have to hope to become well.

———•━•━•———

REFLECT on the Power of Hope

Reflect upon these statements:

- We must choose life or death. Healing—freedom from hope deferred—is a choice that can be made.

- You don't have to be well to hope, but you do have to hope to become well.

APPLY the Power of Hope

What can you begin to hope against hope for? If you feel you have nothing to hope for, look again. What "strings" do you still have left? What in your life is worth living for? Your spouse, your child(ren), a particular cause, a dream, a promise? Write down your thoughts in the back of this book. Now that you've found the music left in you, use these "strings" to begin to sing your song of hope in the night. Invite God's presence to fill the room and begin to speak to and heal your heart.

PRAY the Power of Hope

Father, I thank You for invading my painful, hope-deferred world with a plan to bring me wholeness and peace. I am so grateful that what the enemy meant for evil, You are turning around for good. I repent for wavering in my devotion to You and placing my trust in other things. Today I choose to live, I choose to heal, and I choose to anchor my soul to You, Lord. And in spite of the impossibility of my situation, I will hope anyway.

SCRIPTURES TO READ: Deuteronomy 30:19; Genesis 5:20; Habakkuk 3:17–19; Job 35:10; Psalm 42:8; Acts 16:25; Hebrews 6:18–20

Chapter Six

WINTER IS OVER

IN THE PREVIOUS chapter I discussed the fact that healing from the heart disease associated with hope deferred begins with a choice. It will actually be a series of choices. I'm not implying that you are healing yourself by simply changing the way you think. God wants to heal your wounds, not hide them under a cloak of denial. He wants to cure your heart, not bury your pain. Right choices allow Him to do so.

I used Gideon as one example in the last chapter. I will look further at him here, mentioning two more choices he had to make in order to overcome his hopelessness and its resulting heart disease. To fully understand these choices, a historical context is necessary.

Israel had become an idolatrous nation, worshipping idols and false gods as well as Jehovah. Gideon's family was no exception—the village shrine and altar of worship to Baal and Asherah were in his backyard! Baal was considered a god of fertility, rain (and therefore vegetation), sun, and war.[1] Asherah was a goddess associated with passion and the sea. According to some, she was the wife of El and the mother of Baal.[2] The worship of Baal involved gross immorality, the cutting of one's body, and even child sacrifices. It was hideously evil.

Israel had transferred their trust from Jehovah to these false gods, worshipping them in order to receive the benefits they were believed to provide. In essence, the Israelites were declaring, "Since You haven't come through for us, Jehovah, we're going to put our trust in Baal and Asherah for some of the things we need."

CHOOSING TO TURN FROM IDOLS

The first decision with which God confronted Gideon involved turning from idols. The Lord told Gideon to tear down the altars of Baal and the Asherah pole. "I want to heal you," God was telling Gideon, "but first you must transfer all faith and allegiance to Me."

Though fearful, Gideon obeyed, doing so secretly in the middle of the night due to his fear of the village's reaction. He may not have been completely courageous and full of faith, but Gideon had enough to get started.

In Gideon's act of obedience the next step in your healing process can be seen: *placing your complete hope and trust in God.* Anything in which you have placed your trust, other than God, must be brought under Him. Certainly anything idolatrous must be "torn down," but often idolatry is much more subtle than that. Often it is a transference of trust: "Since God didn't come through, I'll look elsewhere." The mortar for these "elsewhere" altars can be fear, unbelief, past wounds, rejection, bitterness, and a host of other things. Anything associated with hope deferred can be put on the list.

This altar you have bowed to must come down. Every fear, every wall you've put up to protect your heart, every place where you've decided—even if it was unconsciously—that you won't trust God, must come down. Every subtle determination to no longer believe, every testimonial to disappointment that has become a memorial in your heart—*choose now, by faith, to tear it down.* You must do this, not because God is angry with you, but to make way for Him to

become Jehovah Shalom—the Lord of wholeness—
to you.

CHOOSING TO OFFER GOD YOUR PAIN

This will lead you to the next choice God will offer
you. The subsequent event in Gideon's story is so
encouraging it's almost too good to be true. The Lord
instructed Gideon to use the wood from the torn-
down shrines to Baal and Asherah, and build a fire
on which to offer Him a sacrifice.

> *Every fear, every wall you've put up to
> protect your heart must come down.*

Notice, He didn't say burn the idol altars and
then offer Him a sacrifice. No, He said to use the
wood *for* the sacrifice. Please don't miss this. God
was demonstrating to Gideon, and to you as well,
"I won't waste your pain, disillusionment, hopelessness, or even your misplaced trust. Yes, I intend to
remove them, but in the process I want to use them
as a part of your transformation. Worship Me as you
destroy them; let them become part of your offering
to Me. Give Me the pain, the fear. When you trust
Me enough to worship Me even in your pain, this is
an amazing worship. As you do, I will accept it and

cause your destruction of them to light a new fire in you."

Imagine that: God using even your wounds and their debilitating results. Too good to be true? No. He wants to use everything—even your wounds, mistakes, failures, and losses—and transform them into altars of worship. Scripture tells us that God overcomes evil with good and makes even the wrath of man praise Him (Ps. 75:10; Rom. 12:21). What a promise! He is not only bigger than your wounds, losses, fears, and unbelief, but He is also bigger than your mistakes and failures. The Bible is filled with examples of people who have made very serious errors, and yet God was able to redeem and heal. He is merciful and able to deliver you from the pain caused by others and that which you've brought upon yourself.

Jesus accepted the title of "Son of David," even though it made Him "Son" of an adulterer and murderer. Abraham made some very grave mistakes, yet the end result of his life was that he was called the friend of God. The disciples abandoned Jesus at His greatest hour of need, and a few days later they became the leaders of His new movement. Peter denied the Lord with a curse, yet a few days later he was used to heal a lame man and preach a sermon that caused three thousand people to come to Christ. God can and does redeem us from our past.

YOUR SEASON IS CHANGING!

People sometimes refer to their difficult times as "winter seasons." There is a beautiful picture associated with this in Ezekiel 47. The prophet Ezekiel was given a vision of the river of God. In this vision the river produced life and healing everywhere it went. Interestingly, the Hebrew word for "river" in the passage is *nachal,* and means "a stream, especially *a winter torrent.*"[3] Some streams and rivers are dry during certain times of the year. They fill up, however, when there is rain, or, as in this case, the spring thaw melts the snow and ice on the mountains. Tiny rivulets develop, coming together to form streams and, eventually, becoming *nachalim* (rivers). Though Ezekiel's "winter river" began as a trickle in verse 1, it eventually became a mighty, unfordable river by verse 5.

As your season changes, God's healing will likely begin as a mere trickle. You can be confident, however, that it will deepen, that God will use the snow and ice of your spiritual winter to bring a deep flow of His Spirit to you. Your season is changing!

- For those who are confused and disillusioned...

- For the heart grieving from pain and loss...

- For the faithful but weary soldier whose streambed is dry... For those who have lost their first love connection to Him...

- For the Gideon's of the world who are heartsick with hope deferred...your season is changing.

The warmth of spring is going to do its work, and summer is coming. Thank God winter doesn't last forever. The river of healing will flow to you, and you will drink its healing power. Hope deferred will end. Just as it did for Gideon, despair will yield to His command: "Wholeness to you!"

There really is a song left in you.

A passage in the Song of Solomon also speaks of the end of "winter":

My beloved responded and said to me, "Arise, my darling, my beautiful one, and come along. For behold, the winter is past, the rain is over and gone. The flowers have already appeared in the land; the time has arrived for pruning

the vines, and the voice of the turtledove has
been heard in our land. The fig tree has rip-
ened its figs, and the vines in blossom have
given forth their fragrance. Arise, my darling,
my beautiful one, and come along!"
—SONG OF SOLOMON 2:10–13

You are the darling, the beautiful one He is calling
out of winter!

WORKING THINGS TOGETHER FOR GOOD

Psalm 51 was written by a man experiencing hope
deferred. King David had lost his first-love connection with God, which resulted in sin and a winter
season. The following prayer he offered was answered:
"God, make a fresh start in me, shape a Genesis week
from the chaos of my life.... Bring me back from gray
exile, put a fresh wind in my sails!" (vv. 10, 12, THE
MESSAGE).

God is ready to do just that for you. A fresh
start...a Genesis week...out of exile...a fresh wind—
that's what He wants for you.

After Gideon tore down the altar of Baal, demonstrating a rejection of this idol and a new trust in
God, his name was changed to Jerubbaal, meaning
"Baal conqueror" (Judg. 7:1). What a turnaround! That
can be your complete story as well—conquering

every enemy, overcoming every fear, and complete healing of hope deferred.

A well-known verse in Romans summarizes this truth concerning God taking your pain, hurts, and destruction and bringing good from them. It is actually one of the most famous verses in the entire Bible: "And we know that God causes all things to work together for good to those who love God, to those who are called according to His purpose" (Rom. 8:28). This verse packs an even greater punch than most people realize.

The phrase "work together" is from the Greek word *sunergeo*, from which we get the English words *synergy* and *synergism*. Synergism is "the working together of two or more drugs, muscles, etc., to produce an effect greater than the sum of their individual effects."[4] In choosing this word, God is promising He will take all of the bad, all of the pain, and every attempt of the enemy to destroy your faith—"all things"—and then mix in Himself, infusing these evils with His miraculous power. "I will synergize with them," He says, "and the good in Me will overpower the bad in them." Amazing! Disappointment plus pain plus loss morphs into good when the "plus God" occurs! Believing in that truth alone restores hope.

When complimented on her homemade biscuits by Dr. Harry Ironside, the cook at a popular Christian conference center responded, "Just consider what goes into the making of these biscuits. By itself, the flour doesn't taste good; neither does the baking powder, nor the shortening, nor any other ingredient. However, when I mix them all together and put them in the oven, they're transformed. They come out just right."

Much of life can be tasteless, even bad. But God is able to combine these "ingredients" of our life in such a way that when He is finished, the result is good.[5]

PREGNANT WITH HOPE

It's somewhat like a pregnancy. Very few, if any, of the changes that occur to a woman's body during pregnancy could be described as good. But, oh, the beauty of what is growing inside and will one day be seen!

> I believe that hope deferred is being broken off of you. God has planted His words in your heart and you are now pregnant with hope.

A mother, the instant she knows she is with child, lives her every moment in anticipation of delivery. After a time, her pregnancy means she cannot take a step, make a move, or think a thought that is disassociated from the coming of her child.

In America we are taught to ignore the obvious fact that a woman is with child. In France, however, the case is quite the contrary. If a man is introduced to a woman who is an expectant mother, it is the height of politeness for him to congratulate her. *"Je vous félicite de votre esperance"*—"I congratulate you on your hope"—is a common phrase among the cultured.[6]

I believe that hope deferred is being broken off of you. God has planted His words in your heart and you are now pregnant with hope. Perhaps you are only in the first trimester, most likely not yet enjoying the fruit of conception, but the seed of God's words has been planted. He is mixing Himself into your pain, and you *will* give birth.

I congratulate you on your hope!

―――――•‹•›•―――――

REFLECT on the Power of Hope

In this chapter we identified two choices you will have to make in order to receive healing from the heart disease associated with hope deferred.

- Transfer all faith and allegiance to God.

- Give your pain, disillusionment, hopelessness, and misplaced trust to God so that He can use them as part of your transformation.

APPLY the Power of Hope

In spite of your current pain, take time now to create an altar of worship to God by going through the two steps outlined above. With your own sincere words, express your choice to give Him first place in your life. Then tear down anything idolatrous—anything associated with hope deferred—that is taking up residence within your heart. Lastly, surrender all of your heart to the Lord— the good and bad parts. He wants to use it all to redeem and to heal you.

PRAY the Power of Hope

Father, I thank You for wanting and receiving all of me as part of Your love-driven work of redemption. In laying my life down before You today, Jesus, I am inviting

You to become my Jehovah Shalom—the Lord of wholeness over me. Thank You, God of mercy, for bringing my winter season to an end and releasing Your river of healing to flow in me and eventually through me. New life will come forth; hope deferred will end!

SCRIPTURES TO READ: Romans 12:21; Psalm 75:10; Song of Solomon 2:10–13; Revelation 2:4–5; Psalm 51:10, 12; Romans 8:28

Chapter Seven

TELL YOUR HEART TO BEAT AGAIN

IN HIS BOOK *Lee: The Last Years* Charles Bracelen Flood reports that after the Civil War, Robert E. Lee visited a Kentucky lady who took him to the remains of a grand old tree in front of her house. There she bitterly cried that its limbs and trunk had been destroyed by Northern artillery fire. She looked to Lee for a word condemning the North, or at least sympathizing with her loss.

After a brief silence, Lee said, "Cut it down, my dear, and forget it."[1]

We are in the process of cutting down our trees scarred from the enemy's artillery fire. And though it seems impossible at times, the hope-deferred destruction will be replaced with joy. There is "a time to weep and a time to laugh; a time to mourn and a time to dance" (Eccles. 3:4). Mourning our losses is very often appropriate, but God does promise joy in the morning. The fact that you are seeking healing by reading this book means that most likely it is time for your weeping and mourning to end. Dancing and laughter are in your next season. Rubem Alves once said, "Hope is hearing the melody of the future. Faith is dancing to it."[2]

Hope is coming, and you will dance!

DANCING WITH THE LORD

I love the following narrative about dancing. It is very appropriate for hope-deferred sufferers:

> Imagine you and the Lord Jesus are walking down the road together. For much of the way the Lord's footprints go along steadily, consistently, rarely varying the pace. But your footprints are a disorganized stream of zigzags, starts, stops, turnarounds, circles, departures, and returns. For much of the way it seems to go like this, but gradually your footprints come more in line with the Lord's, soon paralleling His consistently. You and Jesus are walking as true friends!
>
> This seems perfect, but then an interesting thing happens. Your footprints, which

once etched the sand next to Jesus', are now walking precisely in His steps. Inside His larger footprints are your smaller ones; you and Jesus are becoming one.

This goes on for many miles, but gradually you notice another change. The footprints inside the large footprints seem to grow larger. Eventually they disappear altogether. There is only one set of footprints; they have become one. This goes on for a long time, but suddenly the second set of footprints is back.

Zigzags all over the place. Stops. Starts. Gashes in the sand. A veritable mess of prints. This time it seems even worse! You are amazed and shocked. Your dream ends.

You pray, "Lord, I understand the first scene with zigzags and fits. I was a new Christian, and I was just learning. But You walked on through the storm and helped me learn to walk with you."

And He spoke softly, "That is correct."

"And when the smaller footprints were inside of Yours, I was actually learning to walk in Your footsteps; I followed you very closely."

And He answered, "Very good. You have understood everything so far."

"When the smaller footprints grew and

filled in Yours, I suppose that I was becoming like You in every way."

And He beamed. "Precisely."

"So, Lord, was there a regression or something? The footprints separated, and the seeming chaos was worse than the first."

There is a pause as the Lord answers with a smile in His voice, "You didn't know? That was when we danced!"[3]

Even if you're not quite ready to dance, try to at least envision yourself dancing again. Every worthwhile accomplishment starts with vision. As we advance toward our waltz, the writer to the Hebrews gives us insight that will help us.

> Therefore, brethren, since we have confidence to enter the holy place by the blood of Jesus, by a new and living way which He inaugurated for us through the veil, that is, His flesh, and since we have a great priest over the house of God, *let us draw near* with a sincere heart in full assurance of faith, having our hearts sprinkled clean from an evil conscience and our bodies washed with pure water. *Let us hold fast the confession of our hope without wavering,* for He who promised is faithful.
> —HEBREWS 10:19–23, EMPHASIS ADDED

Two important but simple steps toward overcoming hope deferred are found in this passage. God doesn't want to overwhelm us with a lot of theology in order to receive our healing. He keeps it simple. Nonetheless, there is great power to be found in these simple and easily implemented truths. The first of them is to "draw near to God and He will draw near to you" (James 4:8). This is without question the most important step in your healing process. When we position ourselves with the Lord, the circumstances around us lose their power to imprison us. His love and power begin to weaken our prison's hold. Perspective and focus change. Our problems and pain will decrease in comparison to His overwhelming presence. The storms of our lives will no longer define us. He will. The power of such a shift in focus is illustrated in the following story:

> In Robert Louis Stevenson's story of a storm, he described a ship caught off a rocky coast, threatening death to all on board. One of the terrified passengers made his way to the pilothouse, where the pilot was lashed to his post with his hands on the wheel, turning the ship little by little into the open sea. The pilot smiled at the man, who then rushed back to the deck below, shouting, "I have seen the face of the pilot and he smiled. All

is well." The sight of the smiling pilot averted panic and converted despair into hope.[4]

When we draw near to the Lord, we will see Him there at the point of our pain. His presence calms us, bringing reassurance that He can handle the situation and guide us through the troubled waters.

DRAW NEAR TO GOD

One of the ways we draw near, of course, is through simple praise and worship. I realize this may sound simplistic, but don't underestimate its power. True worship is so much more powerful than the average person realizes. I actually believe that any person's life could be radically and forever changed by extreme doses of praise and worship. They are the antidote for depression. Simply applying worship in the same way one would therapy—taking time each day singing and exalting the faithfulness and greatness of God—would create a place for Him to enthrone Himself in our hearts. "Yet You are holy, O You who are enthroned upon the praises of Israel" (Ps. 22:3).

From this place of rule He could and would begin to rule over the areas of hurt that cause our pain. Our emotions were created with the ability to heal when the right conditions exist, just as our bodies were. His presence creates those conditions, and praise and worship invite His presence.

Another form of praise is to exalt God's Word and declare His promises. This too seems simple, but it is very powerful. Use the scriptures at the end of this chapter that speak of God's healing power, His mercy, and His love; then praise Him by declaring these scriptures over yourself. Do this in five- to ten-minute increments several times throughout your day. Psalm 107:20 tells us God's Word is actually a medicine—it will heal your heart.

The psalmist David drew near to God for victory over hope deferred while he was in a cave named Adullam. Before becoming king, he was forced to flee from King Saul, and he found himself an outcast from his homeland, Israel. David made this cave his home for several years. What a hopeless situation! But Psalm 27, written during this painful season, speaks of David drawing near to the Lord in his place of pain:

> One thing I have asked from the LORD, that I shall seek: that I may dwell in the house of the LORD all the days of my life, to behold the beauty of the LORD and to meditate in His temple. For in the day of trouble He will conceal me in His tabernacle; in the secret place of His tent He will hide me; He will lift me up on a rock.
>
> —PSALM 27:4–5

Many other psalms were written during this season of David's life. He made his cave a place of communion, of drawing near to God.

Use this psalm, or perhaps even compose one of your own, to draw near to the Lord. If you move into a season of drawing near to Him during your time of pain, of which simple praise and worship are two keys, you will begin to experience change almost immediately.

HOLD FAST THE CONFESSION OF OUR HOPE

The next simple step to healing found in Hebrews 10 is in verse 23, which tells us to "hold fast the confession of our hope without wavering." This phrase sounds a little theological and complicated. Let's simplify it with a couple of definitions and by rephrasing it. The Greek word for "confession" (*homologia*) means "saying the same thing as." Biblically speaking, confession is simply saying what God says about us in His Word. As simple as this seems, it is a tremendous key to our healing from hope deferred. God's Word is powerful. Speaking it releases that power. Psalm 107:2 says, "Let the redeemed of the LORD say so." The Scriptures tell us that death and life are in the power of our words (Prov. 18:21). Think about that—*death and life are released by what we say*. Make sure the words you speak are life-producing words.

SPEAK TO YOUR HEART

Several years ago my brother was allowed to witness an open-heart surgery. During the procedure the patient's heart had been stopped from beating. When it came time to restart it, despite repeated attempts, the medical staff was unable to cause the heart to beat again. Finally, although the patient was obviously unconscious, the surgeon leaned over and spoke into the patient's ear, "We need your help. We cannot get your heart restarted. Tell your heart to start beating." Incredibly, in that instant, the patient's heart began to beat again! Words are powerful, even when hearing them subconsciously. Though obviously unconscious, this patient heard the words, her spirit gave the command, and her heart began to beat. Yours can beat again too, and something as simple as speaking can help restart it.

Declaring over yourself what God says about you—that you have peace, joy, hope, and a healthy heart—even when your circumstances still seem to contradict Him, may feel like denial. In some ways it is. But there is both good and bad denial. Bad denial is trying to be happy by *burying* our emotions, *acting* as though we're OK when really we're not. A humorous example of this can be seen in the following:

The story is told of a great, never-say-die general who was taken captive and thrown into a deep, wide pit along with a number of his soldiers. In that pit was a huge pile of horse manure.

"Follow me," the general cried to his men as he dove into the pile. "There has to be a horse here somewhere!"[5]

That is bad denial! Another name for it is *false hope*. The only positive thing that can be said about the general's denial is that at least he was enough of a leader to go first. This humorous story illustrates bad denial at its worst; it makes about as much sense as some of the ways we try to bury our emotional pain.

Good denial, however, is different. When, in spite of what you feel or what your circumstances tell you, you choose to believe what God's Word says about you, this is good denial. Actually, this is biblical faith. Faith isn't positive thinking, denying the *reality* of your circumstances; faith is denying these circumstances the *right to remain in control* of your life. This exalts God above your situation, and it changes your perspective.

Maintaining Proper Perspective

Perspective is critical. Actually, when it comes to emotional pain, it isn't what happens to you that controls you and ravages your heart. Rather, it is what you *believe* about the situation that controls you.

> *Faith isn't denying the reality of your circumstances; faith is denying these circumstances the right to remain in control of your life.*

This is why two people can experience a similar trauma, such as rejection, betrayal, or loss, and one can recover quite quickly while the other does not. The person who recovered quickly was able to process the experience—probably because of good assistance—through the eyes of hope and faith. They were probably well anchored to God and others, causing them to maintain hope and believe they would be OK.

Holding fast to what God says about you in the midst of your storm gives you this perspective, enabling you to believe you will be healed and experience a complete recovery. This positions the heart to heal. The following story illustrates this:

On January 13, 1997, Steve Fossett climbed into the cockpit of a hot-air balloon with the ambition of being the first to circle the globe in a balloon. After three days he had crossed the Atlantic and was flying eastward over Africa.

The prevailing wind carried him on a direct course for the country of Libya. But Libya had refused permission to fly in its air space, which meant he could be shot down. Balloons cannot turn; so when a change of direction is needed, they must change altitude to find a crosswind blowing in a different direction.

Fossett dropped 6,300 feet, where a southeast wind blew. He safely skirted Libya, then heated the balloon, rose 10,000 feet and caught an easterly wind, which carried him back on course.

Betrand Piccard, another balloonist, sees a similarity between balloon flight and daily life: "In the balloon you are prisoners of the wind and go only in its direction. But you can change altitude, and when you change altitude, you change direction. You are not a prisoner of the wind, anymore.

Likewise, in life people think they are prisoners of the winds of adversity that blow against them. But they are not. *They can change altitude by changing attitude*, and the new attitude will carry them in a new direction.[6]

How liberating to know you are not a prisoner of the adverse winds. Holding fast to what God says about you is one of the ways you change your attitude. It is an appropriate, biblical denial. Face the wind and boldly declare, "In spite of what the winds of adversity have inflicted on me, I'm going to go in another direction—God's!" Then find the current of the Holy Spirit, which will be what God says about you in His Word, and soar with Him to victory.

I don't want to overload you with technical definitions, but the Greek word from which "holding fast" is translated offers even further confirmation of this. It is a nautical term meaning "to set one's course." The word is used in Acts 27 to describe a boat that "set its course" in a particular direction, despite a fierce storm. Agreeing with and declaring what God says in His Word enables us to overcome the storms of life and remain on the course He has chosen for us.

Determine to draw near to God. In the midst of your pain, run to Him—not from Him. You'll find a warm reception and a loving embrace. Then use the Scriptures I have provided for you and begin to say them over yourself. Tell your heart to beat again. It will, and you will awaken to a new you, ready to get your life back on course.

And yes, one day soon you will dance.

REFLECT on the Power of Hope

Let's reflect upon this passage of scripture from Hebrews 10, which outlines for us three simple yet important steps toward overcoming hope deferred:

Therefore, brethren, since we have confidence to enter the holy place by the blood of Jesus, by a new and living way which He inaugurated for us through the veil, that is, His flesh, and since we have a great priest over the house of God, *let us draw near* with a sincere heart in full assurance of faith, having our *hearts sprinkled clean* from an evil conscience and our bodies washed with pure water. Let us *hold fast the confession of our hope* without wavering, for He who promised is faithful.

—HEBREWS 10:19–23, EMPHASIS ADDED

APPLY the Power of Hope

Here is a list of scriptures to help you draw near to God, and make confessions of hope that will align your thoughts, declarations, and attitude with what God has to say about you. Do this in five- to ten-minute increments several times throughout your day.

SCRIPTURES TO READ: Psalm 103:8; 9:9–10; 33:18–22; 138:7; 89:1–2; Romans 5:5; 8:38–39; Jeremiah 31:3; 29:11; Isaiah 40:29, 31; John 8:36; 1 Corinthians 6:19; 1 Timothy 1:7; Philippians 4:13; 1:6; Romans 8:31; Ephesians 1:7; 2:6, 10; 1 Peter 2:4, 9

PRAY the Power of Hope

Father, I am so grateful for the treasury of tools purposely placed in Your Word for overcoming hope deferred. Your mercy, love, and power are so great that the moment I reposition my heart toward You, You meet me at my point of pain with Your healing presence. Today I choose to draw close to You, and I choose to come into agreement with Your words of life and truth. Come and enthrone Yourself in my heart. No longer will I allow painful circumstances to control my life. I position my heart to heal.

SCRIPTURES TO READ: Ecclesiastes 3:4; Hebrews 10:19–23; Psalm 22:3; 27:4–5; 107:2; Proverbs 18:21

Chapter Eight

MINING THE GOLD

PICTURE, AS THEY say, is worth a thousand words. Knowing this, God sculpted and shaped a vivid picture of hope deferred in the form of a mountain—wouldn't you know it would be a mountain! Rugged. Barren. Its very name, Horeb, means "desolation, a waste place, barrenness, dryness"—all synonyms of hope deferred.

This is the place where Moses ended up for much of his forty-year exile, shoveling dung instead of bathing in royal hot tubs. There can be no more severe case of hope deferred than what Moses experienced, having lost his royal inheritance and, it seemed, his destiny. I realize "it ain't over 'til it's over," but after disappearing for forty years, a dream is usually over.

But thankfully, like many mountains, Horeb had treasure hidden within it. Not only would this barren piece of rock be a picture of exile-induced heart disease, but it would also become a glorious example of *conquered* hope deferred and *healed* heart disease. Horeb gives you a glimpse of life on the other side of your pain. The events associated with this place portray God's amazing ability to heal, restore hope and purpose, and bring beautiful treasure from ugly mountains. *Horeb didn't remain horrible for Moses, and it won't for you either.*

The transformation of Horeb became so complete, its power so harnessed by the hand of God, that it eventually became known as "the mountain of God" (Exod. 3:1). It just doesn't get any better than that! God can so transform the Horeb seasons of your life that one day all you will see when you look back at them is Him. "'I know the plans that I have for you,' declares the LORD, 'plans for welfare and not for calamity to give you a future and *a hope*'" (Jer. 29:11, emphasis added).

There is gold in this mountain, and you will find it!

EMBRACE THE PAIN

This became especially real to me a few years back when I found myself in a season of hope deferred, much of which had been caused by rejection and betrayal. While seeking the Lord for comfort one afternoon, He threw me quite a curve. "I need for you to embrace the pain," He spoke very clearly.

What a strange and seemingly cruel statement to hear from a loving Father, who supposedly had great plans for my welfare and a future filled with hope. I did not realize, however, that God wanted more than to simply *remove* my pain; He also wanted to *use* it.

God never wastes your pain; before He removes it, He makes it serve you. Horeb will become your gym and the pharaoh who sent you there your trainer. And ultimately, like God, whose nature you inherited, you will win. He always wins, and so can you.

I want to be very clear that God wasn't telling me that betrayal is good, nor that He caused it. God doesn't cause evil, but He does make it serve Him— and us. He needed for me to embrace the pain, not so I could hurt, but in order to grab it, wrestle it to the mat, and claim my prize!

God wanted more than to simply remove my pain; He also wanted to use it.

God doesn't call evil good, as some people are prone to do. Pain isn't good; it tells you something is wrong. Death is an enemy. Emotional wounds can break your heart. God doesn't make light of your pain, and He isn't playing weird mind games with you, trying to convince you that bad is good.

He is saying, however, that no matter how great the wound and deep the pain, He knows how to heal and transform it. And not just into scar tissue. He will use its lessons to make you better, healthier, richer, and better positioned for a fulfilling future.

Horeb isn't terminal!

THE POWER OF PERSEVERANCE

Learn these lessons from this ugly mountain, and find the buried treasure you can take from it. One of the first things Horeb will have taught you, and one of the most important, is the power of perseverance. Don't downplay this one—it's huge. Waiting isn't easy, and nothing truer can be said than that waiting is associated with hope deferred. Learning to wait without wavering will make you successful in life. God wants to strengthen your endurance through your experience at Horeb so that you can be like the distance runner who can run long distances without damaging the heart or lungs.

Moses is one of the all-time record holders for waiting. After fleeing from Pharaoh and becoming an object lesson on deferred hopes and diseased hearts for forty years, he found it hard to believe God could ever use him again—let alone awaken his dreaming heart. But after a season of arguing with God on this mountain (Exod. 3–4), he decided to give it a try and became the all-time greatest poster boy for restored hope. Sometimes the perceived death of a vision is really just waiting for its divine time! That's why persistence is so crucial.

This could prove to be one of the greatest assets you'll mine from this mountain. Rich DeVos, cofounder of Amway and owner of the Orlando Magic basketball team, says of persistence:

> Persistence is the single most important ingredient of success in life....When confronted with a failure or disappointment, you have only two choices: You can give up, or you can persist....If I could pass on one character trait to young people in the world—one single quality that would help them achieve success in life—it would be persistence. It's more important than intellect, athletic ability, good looks or personal magnetism. Persistence comes from a deep place in the soul. It is a God-given compensation for what we lack in other areas of our life. Never underestimate its power.[1]

YOU OWN A RIGHT TIME

All great men and women have learned to persevere. Galatians 6:9 encourages us to do so without losing heart: "Let us not lose heart in doing good, for in *due time* we will reap if we do not grow weary" (emphasis added).

> *Sometimes the perceived death of a vision is really just waiting for its divine time!*

Sometimes, like Moses, your wait is because you have not yet arrived at God's "due time." The words "due time" in this verse come from the Greek phrase "*idios kairos*" and, when fully understood, are filled with reason to persevere. *Kairos* means "the *right* time; the *opportune* point in time at which something should be done." The second word, *idios*, denotes "ownership."

This verse is telling you to not lose heart while waiting for something God has promised you, because you *own* a *right time* for the promise to arrive. Knowing this sure does make waiting easier.

Elijah is another great leader who had to learn from Horeb. One of the things I love about the Bible is that God gets so "real" with us regarding His leaders. Whether it's David with Bathsheba, Samson with Delilah, or Peter's string of profanity as he denies being one of Christ's followers, God airs the bad as well as the good. We live in a fallen world where mortals mess up, heroes fall off of their pedestals, and real problems come to real people.

How gracious of God to keep it real!

Elijah was one of those "real" heroes in the Bible. He didn't commit adultery and, so far as we know, didn't deny knowing God in between curses. But he did succumb to hope deferred, sink into a dark hole of depression, and have suicidal thoughts. (See 1 Kings 19:1–4.)

I'm not sure how a person with Elijah's level of power—holding back rain, releasing it again after three years, calling down fire from heaven, outrunning a chariot for twenty miles—goes to this level of depression in a matter of days. But he did, and I'm glad God told us about it. If God hadn't told us, we wouldn't have known He took Elijah to Horeb to break the hope-deferred heart disease off of him.

"Get him over where I resurrected Moses's calling," God told the angels. "We'll fix him there." (See 1 Kings 19:5–8.)

And that's exactly what they did.

We're not told why God chose Horeb, but I like to think one of the reasons was to demonstrate—as He did with Moses—His ability to transform defeat into victory. Remember, Horeb means "desolation, barrenness." Perhaps God was thinking, "What a great situation in which to demonstrate once again My power over hopelessness."

After Elijah made it to Horeb, he found himself in a cave. Many scholars believe this was the same cave, or cleft of rock, that Moses was in when God passed before him revealing His glory. (See Exodus 33:19–23.) Some scholars even believe Elijah was aware of this. Maybe God was reminding Elijah of Moses's story, of how He transformed his desolation into hope, his barrenness into fruitful service. Who knows? Perhaps there was even some residue of glory still lingering in the cave! One thing is certain: Elijah arrived in a state of depression and left in a state of victory.

IMPREGNATED WITH HOPE

There is more similarity between the experiences of Elijah and Moses than just the cave. First Kings 19:11 says the Lord was "passing by [*abar*]" Elijah. This word, *abar*, is the same word used when the Lord "passed by" Moses, revealing His glory to him.

Basically the word means to move from one place to another. Sometimes *abar* is a very generic word indicating a *passing into* or *crossing over* from one place to another; it is used this way hundreds of times in the Old Testament. At other times, however, the word carries more weight, signifying a very significant passing into or crossing over, such as Israel crossing the Jordan or Abraham crossing into his inheritance.

Because *abar* means to cross into, it can also mean "to penetrate,"[2] as in penetrating territory, or even the human heart. And since it means penetrate, it is also one of the words used for the physical relationship between a husband and wife. The word can mean "to impregnate."[3] Thinking of this in spiritual terms means that when God penetrates your heart with His Spirit and word, you become "pregnant," carrying His revelation and life. This confirms what I said in chapter 6 about being pregnant with hope.

When God spoke to Elijah at Horeb in "the sound of a gentle whisper" (1 Kings 19:12, TLB), the seed of His word impregnated the discouraged prophet. Elijah became pregnant with renewed hope. But something else was also deposited in Elijah. He received an increased anointing to impart to Elisha, Jehu, and Hazael, men who would eventually finish the work of transforming Israel.

What a turnaround! At Elijah's darkest hour one word from God impregnated him with the power to birth three of Israel's future leaders. God can change things quickly. In His presence weakness gives way to strength.

> *Pain is inevitable; suffering is optional.*

God wants to do this for you as well. At your Horeb, in your place of hope deferred, even in a season of desolation and great despair, God will speak to you. When He does, you'll become "pregnant" with what you need to finish your race. Listen closely, for as it was with Elijah, the voice of hope often comes in a gentle whisper.

God knows when you need His thunderous voice that sounds like many waters, and He knows when you need the gentle whisper. Our Father knows when you need Him to come as the great Lion of Judah, but He understands that at other times you need Him to descend in the form of a dove. He will come in the way you need Him. His plan is to speak a word into your heart that will impregnate you with the courage and faith you need in order to overcome any setback life can dish out.

After suffering severe burns on his legs at the age of five, Glenn Cunningham was given up on by doctors who believed he would...spend the rest of his life in a wheelchair....

The doctors examined his legs, but they had no way of looking into Glenn Cunningham's heart. He didn't listen to the doctors and set out to walk again. Lying in bed...Glenn vowed, "Next week, I'm going to get out of bed. I'm going to walk." And he did just that.

His mother tells of how she used...to look out the window to watch Glenn reach up and take hold of an old plow in the yard. With a hand on each handle, he began to make his gnarled and twisted legs function. And with every step a step of pain, he came closer to walking. Soon he began to trot; before long he was running....

"I always believed that I could walk, and I did. Now I'm going to run faster than anybody has ever run." And did he ever.

He became a great miler who, in 1934, set the world's record of 4:06. He was honored as the outstanding athlete of the century at Madison Square Garden.[4]

Someone once said that pain is inevitable; suffering is optional. Glen Cunningham moved on from Horeb. You can as well!

Choose now to get off of this mountain. Mine the gold of endurance, receive the impartation God wants to deposit in you, and move on. Don't allow Horeb to define you, only to make you better.

And pregnant.

———•••••———

REFLECT on the Power of Hope

At Elijah's darkest hour one word from God impregnated him with the power to impact three of Israel's future leaders. God can change things quickly. In His presence weakness gives way to strength. God wants to do this for you as well. At your Horeb, in your place of hope deferred, even in a season of desolation and great despair, God will speak to you. When He does, you'll become "pregnant" with what you need to finish your race.

APPLY the Power of Hope

Find a solitary place, where you can position your heart before the Lord each day. Wait silently before Him, and listen closely for His voice. As it was with Elijah, the voice of hope often comes in a gentle whisper. Journal what the Lord speaks to your heart. As you learn to wait on Him more and more, He will penetrate your heart with His Spirit and word of hope, strengthening your endurance and impregnating you with His revelation and life.

PRAY the Power of Hope

Father, I thank You for taking the worst experiences of my life and transforming them into life lessons that will make me better, healthier, richer, stronger, and position me for a fulfilling future. Lord, teach me to wait in Your presence until I am impregnated with identity, purpose, destiny, and courage for the road ahead. Teach me to wait without wavering on my Horeb, until dead dreams and visions receive new life. Thank You, Lord, for determining a right time for my promise to arrive. You are forever faithful. None who wait on You will be ashamed. My soul waits for You.

SCRIPTURES TO READ: Galatians 6:9; Jeremiah 29:11; Habakkuk 2:2–3; Psalm 25:3; 27:14; 33:7, 9; 40:1; 130:5–6; Isaiah 25:9; 30:18; 40:30–31; 64:4

Chapter Nine

FRESH START MOUNTAIN

O NE OF THE negative side effects of hope deferred can be a loss of confidence. This is especially true when you feel that your own decisions have created the situation. The resulting lack of belief in your ability becomes a straitjacket, binding your creativity and paralyzing you with fear. Moses, the great leader of Israel during the exodus from Egyptian slavery, is a prime example.

Once upon a time, in what seemed like a fairy-tale life, Moses was filled with self-confidence. And why not? Saved from infanticide, pulled from a basket on the bank of the Nile, adopted by the daughter of a king, and raised in a palace—Moses lived in a bubble where he had everything going for him. But the bubble started weakening when he discovered he wasn't really an Egyptian. It began leaking air when he killed an Egyptian in order to defend an Israelite. And it finally burst when he was forced to flee for his life to Midian. So much for fairy tales.

Moses seemed to adjust fairly well, accepting his fate and creating a decent life in Midian. He found a wife, started a family, and became a rancher. After forty years Moses seemed to have lived a contented life. But that all changed on one of his visits to Horeb. A bush started burning without being consumed. Moses began hearing a voice speak from it, and the quiet life of a has-been dreamer was rudely interrupted.

"Go back to Egypt," the voice said, "and set My people free from their slavery in Egypt." (See Exodus 3:6–10.)

One can only imagine the shock Moses must have felt. The assignment may have surprised him more than the talking, flame-resistant bush. And when he finally realized this really was God talking to him, Moses's responses were very revealing.

> But Moses said to God, "Who am I, that I should go to Pharaoh, and that I should bring the sons of Israel out of Egypt?"
> —Exodus 3:11

Then Moses said to the LORD, "Please, Lord, I have never been eloquent, neither recently nor in time past, nor since You have spoken to Your servant; for I am slow of speech and slow of tongue.... Please, Lord, now send the message by whomever You will."

—Exodus 4:10–13

Moses's self-confidence had been crushed by the events of forty years ago. Trained as a leader by the finest minds of Egypt, he now felt confidence only with sheep. "Leave the nation leading to others," he thought. "I laid down that dream a long time ago."

But God persisted with a few more miracles and some very revelatory dialogue, and the rest, as they say, is history. Moses did, indeed, go back to Egypt and was used by God to deliver a nation from four hundred years of slavery to become what was then the most powerful nation on earth.

GOD'S EXQUISITE IRONY

Can you imagine anything more ironic than God using a mountain, the name of which means "desolation or barrenness," to picture new beginnings? God transformed Horeb into "Fresh Start Mountain"!

God can metamorphose the pain of hope deferred into such wholeness that Horeb, as impossible as it sounds, becomes a place of new beginnings. It was on this mountain that Moses's calling was restored (Exod. 3–4). He no doubt believed his destiny was lost forever. And no place could have been a more accurate picture of his life story than this very mountain where he worked tending sheep. It must have been a constant reminder to Moses of his hope deferred, adding insult to injury: "Not only is my life Horeb, but I work there."

Moses was so filled with hopelessness that in these two chapters God never was fully able to bring him to a place of believing in his renewed calling. He consistently insisted to the Lord that he was not qualified and didn't want to do it. Finally God simply said, "I've heard enough! You are going to do this." (See Exodus 4:10–17.)

God cares more about our destinies than we do!

GET THE FIRE ALIVE AGAIN!

In the New Testament the apostle Paul's spiritual son, Timothy, was discouraged. Timothy was a young man who found himself leading a large congregation through very tough times. Timothy's hope deferred had shut down his gifts. Paul told Timothy to "kindle afresh" his gifts (2 Tim. 1:6). The Greek word translated as "kindle afresh" is filled with insight. *Anazoporeo*, the word Paul used, is actually composed of three Greek words: *Ana* means "again";

zo traces back to *zao*, from which we get the concept of being "alive"; and *pureo* is from *pur*, meaning "fire or lighting." The message this word carries doesn't translate easily. It means to "get the fire alive again," or "get the life in you hot again."

> *God cares more about our destinies than we do!*

"I need your gifts to come alive again!" he said to Timothy. "I need passion to come alive, which will light the flame of your giftings."

When the fire goes out, your gifts go with it.

Paul reminded Timothy that he had been called "with a holy calling…according to [God's] own purpose and grace" (2 Tim. 1:9). *Purpose* (*prothesis*) means "the setting forth of someone's purpose (*thesis*) in advance (*pro*)." God has a destiny for us, and He is committed to its fulfillment. He is the beginning, the end, and, when necessary, a renewing in between! But there is more to *prothesis*.

Prosthesis is an English word derived from this Greek word. A prosthesis is an artificial body part, such as an arm or leg, constructed to restore purpose to that which was lost. Paul was encouraging his spiritual son Timothy, saying, "Hey, man, don't forget that God gave you a destiny. And when life seems to have cut off that purpose, He can restore it. Now, start burning the flame again!"

The great verse in Romans 8:28 uses *prothesis*. "And we know that God causes all things to work together for good to those who love God, to those who are called according to His purpose." This verse is saying that no matter what part of our purpose has been cut off, God has already prepared the prosthesis that will restore it. What a great promise for those suffering from hope deferred.

Horeb, as much as any other place on earth, illustrates this fact. There, new beginnings are brought forth from the ashes of desolation and hope-deferred pain. In this barren place we discover that God is bigger than our enemies, our mistakes, sins, shortcomings, and fears. There is hope, even at Horeb.

HOPE AND LIFE IN JESUS CHRIST

A dear friend and powerful intercessor who has been mightily used of God over the world experienced a fresh start at her Horeb many years ago. I would not ordinarily include such a lengthy testimony, but Barbara Byerly's story is such a beautiful account of the transforming power of God. Enjoy.

> There's not a pretty way to say it. I was twenty-eight years old and miserable. My marriage was falling apart after ten years. We

had three small sons, and I'd lost two babies in miscarriages. My semi-invalid mother-in-law, Maggie, lived with us and required considerable care. My father had just died, and I was flying from New Jersey to Texas for his funeral. I had lost the capacity to love and couldn't overcome the stress in my life. I felt as if I were living with a bag over my head and couldn't breathe.

As I traveled alone to my father's funeral, a Japanese man seated next to me on the plane initiated conversation and eventually asked, "Do you know my Jesus?"

What a question to ask *me*! I was an American woman who had always gone to church. I turned away, contemplating the turn of events in my life. I would soon see my mother, who had just been released from another stay in a mental hospital, as well as other family members, many of whom had helped raise my siblings and me during my mom's numerous hospitalizations. During the next few days the Japanese traveler's question haunted me. *Did I know Jesus?*

After I returned home, I began to seek counsel from my pastor. We had agreed to meet for six sessions in mid-April, and I had told him about my plan to take the boys and leave my husband in June. On June 8 I entered the pastor's office for my last counseling session. He had attempted to reveal truth to me during our previous meetings, but I was living in darkness, unable to receive light.

Suddenly, without thinking about it, I blurted out, "A man seated next to me on the plane as I was flying to my daddy's funeral asked me if I knew Jesus. The question is haunting me. Do you think I know Jesus?"

My pastor must have been shocked. I was a Sunday school teacher and president of the women's group at our church. Jim and I were both active in our congregation, and on the surface our lives would look good. But I knew I was like the "whitewashed tombs" Jesus described in Matthew 23:27—beautiful on the outside, but inside full of dead men's bones and uncleanness.

I can't fully explain what happened in the next few moments after my question, but the light of God's glory supernaturally filled the pastor's office. I suddenly saw myself a sinner in need of a Savior and began crying out to Him. The Lord miraculously set me free of fear and bitterness, while His love and grace enveloped me. I picked up a Bible, and it opened to Deuteronomy 30:19, "I have set before you life and death...choose life."

"I choose life!" I blurted out in front of my shocked pastor.

I left that room a transformed woman. Even the world around me seemed to be bursting forth in Technicolor. I realized I had been in such darkness that I had not seen spring arrive. When I reached the house, I raced up to my mother-in-law's room, excited to tell someone what had happened to me. As I shared with her, God's miraculous love healed us both—her of a cardiovascular infirmity that had made her an invalid for nine years, and me of debilitating resentment and bitterness. My marriage began afresh too as I fell in love again with the special guy I had married. God's amazing grace transformed our lives.[1]

As long as Jesus lives, there is always hope. The psalmist said we pass through the valley of Baca (weeping), not that it is our permanent abode. (See Psalm 84:6.) I know you have waited—some of you a long time—but like Barbara, you can choose life. And by the way, it was Moses who challenged Israel to choose life with those words in Deuteronomy. "I chose life after forty years of lost hope," he must have been thinking. "If I can do it, so can you."

Listen to the God of Horeb, and choose life.

You too have the power to choose life. In the midst of your pain, you still possess the power to choose. It may seem difficult, but it will be worth it. You will step into a new day and a new life.

Your fresh start is waiting.

———•••———

REFLECT on the Power of Hope

God not only wants to bring forth new beginnings from the ashes of desolation and hope-deferred pain, but He also wants to reveal Himself to us in the process. As the Japanese traveler did of my friend Barbara, ask yourself, "Do I really know Jesus? In what ways have I yet to know Him? As my provider? As my comforter? As my hope?" Use the journal section in the back of this book to make note of all that God whispers to your heart.

APPLY the Power of Hope

Using the responses you've noted, take time right now, as well as in your daily devotionals, to invite Jesus to become something new for you. Invite Him in this new season to become what He hasn't been for you in the past due to sin or sickness of heart.

PRAY the Power of Hope

Thank You, Father, for entering into the whitewashed tomb of my hope-deferred heart with Your gifts of new life, revived destiny, and renewed relationship with You. I am grateful for Your commitment to my destiny and for Your desire to fan into flame the gifts and calling You've placed within me. I choose to embrace the thoughts and plans You have for me; plans to prosper me, to give me hope and a bright future. Take me from hope deferred to wholeness, Lord, for today I choose life!

SCRIPTURES TO READ: Matthew 23:27; Psalm 46:10; Deuteronomy 30:19–20; Jeremiah 29:11; 2 Timothy 1:9

Chapter Ten

THE STAFF OF GOD

Billy Graham had a friend who lost his job, wife, and home during the Great Depression. But this man tenaciously held to his faith—the only thing he had left. One day he stopped to watch some men doing stonework on a huge church. One of them was chiseling a triangular piece of stone. "What are you going to do with that?" asked his friend. The workman said, "See that little opening away up there near the spire? Well, I'm shaping this down here, so it will fit in up there."

Tears filled his eyes as he walked away, for it seemed that God had spoken through the workman to explain the ordeal through which he was passing, "I'm shaping you down here so you'll fit in up there."[1]

Yes, God is shaping you for "up there." But not just for up there. He is also shaping you for your future down here. God will allow the chisel called "Horeb," however, to chip off only your rough edges. Your strength will remain, and you will find your niche in His kingdom.

HOREB-DERIVED WEAPONS

God is using your hope deferred to shape more than you, however. He is also shaping some of the tools you'll need in your future. You will leave Horeb better equipped than when you arrived.

It was on this mountain that God asked Moses, "What is that in your hand?" (Exod. 4:2). Moses held a simple staff used for walking and tending sheep; the Hebrew word is *matteh*,[2] which is also the word for a scepter. Moses's "scepter" was a crooked, knobby, dead piece of wood shaped by the adverse climate on the mountain of desolation. Ultimately, however, the staff of Horeb became known as "the staff of God" (v. 20). Now there's a transformation for you.

God didn't want Moses to carry a polished, gold-plated, gem-studded scepter from Egypt as the symbol of his heavenly authority. Yahweh wanted something depicting the strength of character that only the wind, sun, rain, and snow of Horeb could create. "I took from you the golden scepter of Egypt,"

God was demonstrating, "and gave you one symbolizing brokenness, meekness, and no confidence in the flesh. It has, indeed, been a staff of hope-deferred desolation, but now I am transforming it into My scepter of authority. Your brokenness will become your strength, and your meekness will produce a confidence in Me."

In Exodus 4:17 God declared, "Take this staff in your hand so you can perform miraculous signs *with it*" (NIV, emphasis added). With that ugly stick representing brokenness, meekness, and confidence in God alone, Moses judged nations, parted seas, and brought forth water from a rock. It is your brokenness—even your failure—God uses to prepare you for great authority, not your strengths. What an encouraging truth.

On one occasion when Israel was attacked by a group known as the Amalekites (Exod. 17), God's plan for victory was to use this memento from Horeb. Moses was instructed to take "the staff of God" onto a nearby mountain and hold it over the battlefield. The divine authority represented by this staff enabled Joshua and his army to defeat their enemy. What a powerful picture—God using a Horeb-produced "weapon" to conquer enemies. Hope-deferred mountains can become weapon factories!

LITTLE ANNIE'S PRISON OF HOPE

This concept is amply illustrated by the story of a girl named Little Annie. Although she didn't know it at the time, her place of utter hopelessness provided the tools she would need in her future:

> In an asylum dealing with severely disturbed individuals was a girl called Little Annie. Totally unresponsive to the staff's many attempts at helping her, she was finally confined to a cell in the basement of the asylum and given up as a hopeless case.
>
> One of the workers, however, spent her lunch hours in front of Little Annie's cell, reading to her and praying that God would free her from her prison of silence. Day after day, this woman came to Little Annie's door; but the little girl, however, made no response.
>
> Then, many months later, Little Annie began to speak. Amazingly, within two years she was told she could leave the asylum and enjoy a normal life. Little Annie, however, chose not to leave, and instead stayed to work with the other patients.
>
> Nearly half a century later, at a special ceremony honoring her life, Helen Keller was asked what she credited for her success at overcoming her handicaps. Her reply? "If it

hadn't been for Ann Sullivan, I wouldn't be here today."

Ann Sullivan, who tenaciously loved and believed in an incorrigible blind and deaf girl named Helen Keller, was Little Annie.[3]

> *It is your brokenness—even your failure—God uses to prepare you for great authority, not your strengths.*

Annie's experiences in an asylum of hopelessness equipped her to bring transformation to Helen Keller's world. What might God want to put in your hands through your place of brokenness? Character? Courage? Understanding? When you have conquered this mountain, you will find that it has rewarded you with a new strength and authority.

The Reward of Increased Authority

One of the authority-increasing benefits you will leave with is a greater understanding of God and His ways. He wants you to leave this season knowing Him more intimately. Consider the following examples of God revealing Himself on Horeb:

- Moses received the revelation of God as "I Am That I Am" (Exod. 3:14, KJV).

- Israel received the revelation that He is Jehovah Nissi, which means the Lord is our banner and victory, the One who fights our battles for us (Exod. 17:15).

- The Lord visited Moses, showing him His goodness and glory (Exod. 33:19–23).

I love Exodus 19:17, which states, "And Moses brought the people out of the camp *to meet God*, and they stood at the foot of the mountain" (emphasis added). What a thought—stand at the bottom of Desolation Mountain and meet with God! Yes, you can meet and know Him in new ways as you walk through hope deferred. It may not be a burning bush or a shaking mountain, but you will experience God and His faithfulness in new ways at Horeb. And when you do, the new revelations of His nature and His Father heart will become sustaining forces in your future.

Consider Joseph's journey through hope deferred— slavery, imprisonment in Egypt, and forgotten by those he helped. But God was faithful, and finally Joseph became the second most powerful man in Egypt. "Your brothers intended to *dislocate* you; I used it to *relocate* you," was God's final verdict. Only on the other side of hope deferred, however, did this

revelation come. Eventually God used Joseph to pre-
serve the nation of Israel in a time of famine. When
allowed to, God always turns the tables on Horeb.

God's Plan for Your Pain

Perhaps Satan has intended to make you an outcast—
God will make you a healer of outcasts. Maybe a
deathbed robbed you of a loved one—God will use
you to bring healing to those in grief. There are
always two plans for your difficult times—Satan's
plan in causing them and God's plan of redeeming
them. Satan's plan is usually obvious: heart failure.
He wants you to give up, retreat from life, and turn
from God. God's plan, however, isn't often seen until
you emerge on the other side of the pain.

It is doubtful that Susanna Wesley, in the midst
of her horrible circumstances, could have ever imag-
ined the incredible purpose God had for two of her
children:

> Susanna Annesley was born in 1669, the last
> of twenty-five children. Married to Samuel
> Wesley, she gave birth to nineteen children,
> nine of whom died in infancy. Her life was
> turbulent, frequently unhappy, and filled
> with trials.
>
> Samuel was often gone from home, leaving
> her alone and almost penniless to care for

her family. Unable to properly manage his small salary, he was put in debtor's prison for a time. They disagreed on many points in both politics and religion, resulting in further separation and conflicts.

The Wesleys lived in impoverished circumstances; at one point their home burned to the ground. Susanna suffered from many illnesses and was often bedridden, requiring household help. Between 1697 and 1701 Susanna gave birth to five babies, including twins, all of whom died. Three children later, in 1705, an exhausted nursemaid rolled over onto the newest baby and suffocated it. Many of her children who did live were so errant that they caused her considerable grief.

Yet, her sons John and Charles became two of the greatest evangelists of all time, and their ministry shook the world.[4]

There are always two plans for your difficult times—Satan's plan in causing them and God's plan of redeeming them.

Your Horeb may seem so devastating and painful that you can't see how anything good could possibly come from it. But God does have a plan, and He will bring about His redemptive purposes in your life. Don't give up. One day you will find the scepter He's shaping for you on your mountain of desolation.

Hope!

REFLECT on the Power of Hope

There are always two plans for our difficult times—Satan's plan is causing it, and God's plan is redeeming it. What areas of your life do you believe God wants to redeem? What might God want to derive from your place of hope-deferred desolation to place as a staff of authority in your hands? Journal what comes to mind.

APPLY the Power of Hope

Right now, as well as in your daily devotional times, take some time to place your list of redemptive areas as an offering before the Lord. Invite God to carry out His redemptive purposes for your life. You may use the following scriptures or others that you look up, as well as your own words to express your heart to God.

SCRIPTURES TO READ: Ephesians 1:7; Titus 2:14; 1 Peter 1:18–19; Psalm 130:7; Isaiah 43:1–2; Philippians 1:6; 3:13–14; Ezekiel 36:26; Psalm 51:10–13; 139:23–24; 119:154; 26:11; Romans 8:17–18, 28; Ephesians 1:11; 2 Corinthians 5:17; 14:17–18

PRAY the Power of Hope

Your mercy and loving-kindness, God, are amazing! Truly You work all things for my good and for Your redemptive purposes. Father, You delight in converting my hope-deferred mountains into weapons factories! You also reward my mountain conquering with a greater understanding of Your heart and ways and with new strength and new levels of authority. I am so grateful for the redemptive, sustaining work You are performing in and through me. Today, Lord, I give You my heart, and I fully surrender.

SCRIPTURES TO READ: Exodus 4:2, 17, 20; Ephesians 1:7; Psalm 130:7; Philippians 1:6; Ezekiel 36:26; Psalm 51:10; 139: 34–24

Chapter Eleven

THE HOLY PLACE

O NE OF THE more spectacular events associated with Horeb occurred in Exodus 17. Israel was in desperate need of water. Those who have experienced the pain of hope deferred know it can be a very dry place. God said, "Take your scepter, Moses—the old, weather-beaten staff I fashioned for you on Desolation Mountain—and strike this rock." That must have taken some faith! But Moses did it. He smote the rock, and enough water began gushing forth to satisfy several hundred thousand people. An underground river must have surfaced. You never know what surprises God has buried on this mountain until you need them.

A RIVER OF LIFE

First Corinthians 10:4 tells us this smitten rock represents Christ, and the water that flowed from it represents the river of life He released at Calvary. Just take a moment and ponder that. The forgiveness of sin, the healing of a broken heart, eternal life—all of the benefits of your salvation—are pictured by this event on Horeb. It is fair to say that not just *in spite of* Horeb, not just *when you leave* Horeb, but *out of* Horeb itself a river of life will flow.

God redeemed this horrible, barren, dry place and transformed it into one from which a life-saving river flowed. He did this to give you a picture of how He would one day transform the "horrible" cross into the most powerful symbol of hope in all of history. Your hope-deferred pain is no match for Him. He will conquer it, just as He did sin and death on the cross.

Isaiah speaks of rivers in the desert (Isa. 43:19–20). Wanting a river in the desert seems like foolish, wishful thinking—almost like Abraham and Sarah hoping against hope for a child while in their nineties. Go ahead and hope, though, because we serve an amazing God, and there will be an Isaac!

You can leave hope deferred with a greater dimension of the power and anointing of the Holy Spirit—the river of God—as shown in the following story:

Poor health haunted Dr. A. B. Simpson, and a physician told him he would never live to be forty. This diagnosis underscored the physical helplessness the minister knew all too well. Preaching was an agonizing effort. Walking was painful, and climbing even a slight elevation brought on a suffocating agony of breathlessness.

In desperation, sick in body and despairing in spirit, Dr. Simpson went to his Bible. As he studied, he became convinced that Jesus intended healing to be part of the redemption of humankind's total being. He prayed, asking Christ to fulfill all the needs of his body, until his life's work was done. Every fiber in him tingled with the sense of God's presence.

During the first three years after this healing, he preached more than a thousand sermons, conducting sometimes as many as twenty meetings in one week. For the rest of his life, he was noted for the amazing volume of his sermonic, pastoral and literary work.

Simpson lived to be seventy-six, but his work has lived after him. The Christian and Missionary Alliance, which he founded, is still a potent spiritual force today; his books are still being published and are blessing millions of people.[1]

At his place of hope deferred, Dr. Simpson drank of the river of life; not only was he revived, but also water from that stream is still flowing and impacting lives today. Allow God to turn your desert into an oasis. Make it serve you!

HOREB: A MOST HOLY PLACE

Finally, one of the most incredible, comforting revelations associated with Horeb is that the desolate place can become the holy place. At Mount Horeb Moses was told, "Remove your sandals from your feet, for the place on which you are standing is holy ground" (Exod. 3:5). Later, the Lord told Moses this mountain was so holy that if any person or animal touched it, they would die:

> You shall set bounds for the people all around, saying, "Beware that you do not go up on the mountain or touch the border of it; whoever touches the mountain shall surely be put to death. No hand shall touch him, but he shall surely be stoned or shot through; whether beast or man, he shall not live."
> —EXODUS 19:12–13

The "Horeb-ble" place became the holy place. God had assured Moses that he would come back to this very mountain and worship (Exod. 3:12). Not, "You shall come back to this *awful* place." Not, "You shall come back to this mountain and *curse* it." No. Horeb was now conquered. God had arrested its power of desolation and barrenness, using it to shape perhaps the greatest leader the world has ever known. And He now called it His mountain, the "mountain of God" (1 Kings 19:8). Now Moses would lead an entire nation back to this holy place and *worship*.

I know that in the horrible, dark night of the soul hope seems impossible. And it is, really. It's just that God does the impossible. He takes the difficult places—the events that brought about your hope deferred—and through His incredible wisdom and power makes them produce something good. So good, in fact, that later you can actually return to them in your heart and worship Him: "God, I don't know how, but in that difficult place You proved Yourself faithful, bringing me life and making me stronger. I worship You."

BEAUTY OUT OF BROKENNESS

Moses must have thought, "For forty years I thought this place was horrible. Now I realize it is holy." Some of the most dramatic encounters and visitations ever experienced with God occurred on this mountain called "Desolation."

Out of your brokenness, out of your place of pain, God knows how to bring healing and make Horeb a place of worship.

At the Royal Palace of Tehran, in Iran, you can see one of the most beautiful mosaic works in the world. The ceilings and walls flash like diamonds in multifaceted reflections.

Originally, when the palace was designed, the architect specified huge sheets of mirrors on the walls. When the first shipment arrived from Paris, they found—to their horror—that the mirrors were shattered. The contractor threw them in the trash and brought the sad news to the architect.

Amazingly the architect ordered all of the broken pieces collected, then smashed them into tiny pieces. Then he glued them to the walls to create a mosaic of silvery, shimmering, mirrored bits of glass.

Broken to become beautiful!

It's possible to turn your shattered image into a shimmering testimony of beauty. It's possible to be better because of brokenness. It is extremely rare to find in the great museums of the world objects of antiquity that are unbroken. Indeed, some of the most precious items in the world are only broken pieces—broken, but beautiful.[2]

Out of your brokenness, out of your place of pain, God knows how to bring healing and make a place of worship.

You may feel that your life has been hopelessly destroyed, but God doesn't feel that way. He knows how to form the broken pieces of your soul into something exquisitely wonderful. Never underestimate His power to repair and restore.

Don't run from Horeb. Stare it in the face and tell it you will win. Tell it your God will prevail, and the two of you will commune together on top of it—not under it.

Then start hoping. Hope again. Dream again. Live again.

I know you can; I believe you will.

———•◦•—

REFLECT on the Power of Hope

Take time to read through and reflect
upon this passage of Scripture. Think of
how it applies to your Horeb:

The Spirit of the Lord God is upon me
Because the LORD has anointed me
To bring good news to the afflicted;
He has sent me to bind up the
        brokenhearted,
To proclaim liberty to captives
And freedom to prisoners;
To proclaim the favorable year of the
    LORD
And the day of vengeance of our God;
To comfort all who mourn,
To grant those who mourn in Zion,
Giving them a garland instead of ashes,
The oil of gladness instead of mourning,
The mantle of praise instead of a spirit
        of fainting.
So they will be called oaks of
        righteousness,

The planting of the Lord, that He may
be glorified.

Then they will rebuild the ancient ruins,
They will raise up the former
devastations;
And they will repair the ruined cities,
The desolations of many generations.
—Isaiah 61:1–4

APPLY the Power of Hope

The verses above describe what God desires to do in your life. Read this passage
over and over again each day—out loud.
Modify the language a bit to specifically
address your circumstances in first person. (i.e., "I will no longer wear ashes of
disappointment on my head, for God is
crowning me with a beautiful garland
of hope-filled dreams!") In doing so, you
will stare Horeb in the face and tell it you
will win, your God will prevail, and the
two of you will commune together on
top of it. Envision what these verses say
God desires to do in and through your
life; start to hope and dream again. Journal what you see.

PRAY the Power of Hope

Who is like You, Lord? Granting forgiveness and grace, crowning me with compassion and loving-kindness, renewing my strength, satisfying me with good things, and doing exquisite wonders on my behalf. Give me eyes to see and ears to hear and to recognize the new thing You are causing to spring forth from my barren place. Lord, lead me to walk on the wilderness pathway You've paved for me. Lead me to drink from the river You're causing to flow from my desert place. In You, Jesus, there is abundant life! My mountain of desolation was so great, but in Your mercy, Lord, You make all things new.

SCRIPTURES TO READ: 1 Corinthians 10:4; Isaiah 43:19–20; 1 Corinthians 2:9; Deuteronomy 29:4; Revelation 3:18; Psalm 103; John 10:10

Chapter Twelve

EXPECT!

FOR THERE IS hope for a tree, when it is cut down, that it will sprout again, and its shoots will not fail. Though its roots grow old in the ground and its stump dies in the dry soil, at the scent of water it will flourish and put forth sprigs like a plant" (Job 14:7–9).

Hope is becoming a reality in you. Even though you may have felt like a tree totally destroyed and cut down, you can now smell water—the water of life—and it is bringing you the power of hope.

You will sing again.

You will dance again.

You will live.

You will climb out of the debris and crow.

By the grace of God and the power of the Holy Spirit, you're going to get busy livin'! You will be like the woman in Mark's gospel who refused to give up:

> A woman who had had a hemorrhage for twelve years, and had endured much at the hands of many physicians, and had spent all that she had and was not helped at all, but rather had grown worse—after hearing about Jesus, came up in the crowd behind Him and touched His cloak.
>
> —MARK 5:25–27

This woman had suffered an ongoing, incurable condition for many years. She was, no doubt, weak from the continual drain on her system. Many doctors—yes, the passage says "many"—had put her through numerous difficult experiences. She had exhausted all of her resources, yet she had grown worse. There was no hope, but still she hoped anyway.

Even though Jewish law forbade anyone in her "unclean" condition to touch others, she wasn't deterred. She wasn't going to miss her opportunity for healing. This lady had more faith in Christ's ability to heal her than she did in her disease's power to defile Him. "I'm going to touch Him," she determined. "I don't care how crowded it is, how far away He is from me, or how many hundreds of people are between us. I don't care who thinks I am breaking the law by touching others and Him. Even if I have to crawl, reach out, and barely touch the hem of His garment, *I am going to get to Jesus and receive my healing.*"

Don't you just love this woman's indomitable spirit? That's what I call the power of hope!

I believe you're going to do that! Deep within you there is a spirit of faith just waiting to be resurrected. Get to Jesus! Whatever it takes, touch Him. Crawl if you have to, but get to Him. Even if you have spent all that you have, and all the doctors, therapists, friends—and anyone else—say there's no hope for you, hope anyway! Push through the fear, pain, confusion, and the mob of circumstances that stand in your way and *get to Jesus.* This is a choice only you can make.

SEEDS OF HOPE

In this chapter I want to encourage your faith by planting specific seeds in you. Hope seeds. Faith seeds. They are simply declarations of biblical promises, chosen to encourage, challenge, and inspire you. Begin to expect these things. Make a conscious choice to believe they are going to happen, and you will partake of hope fulfilled.

Several months before I wrote this book, the Lord awakened Isaiah 59 and 60 in my heart. From them

I have compiled a list of things God wants to do for you. Allow them to encourage your faith. As you take hold of them with your heart and apply them to your life, you will reap a bountiful harvest of hope.

> *Deep within you there is a spirit of faith*
> *just waiting to be resurrected.*

Expect the zeal of the Lord to come to you with justice, salvation, and an outpouring of His Holy Spirit.

Isaiah 59:15–21 shows the intensity with which God desires to bring deliverance. He is zealous for you. Justice and salvation (wholeness) are coming to your life as a holy invasion. His Spirit will be poured out upon you.

The Lord is coming with great zeal. Expect salvation to come to your offspring (Isa. 59:21; 60:4). Expect prodigals to come home. Expect those who are rebellious, addicted, and bound by all manner of sin to be delivered. Salvation is coming to your household. Expect it!

Expect the glory of the Lord to come to and upon you.

Isaiah 60:1 in the Amplified Bible declares: "Arise [from the depression and prostration in which circumstances have kept you—rise to a new life!] Shine (be radiant with the glory of the Lord), for your light has come, and the glory of the Lord has risen upon you!"

The Hebrew word for glory has the meaning of something that is heavy or weighty. The Greek concept is to recognize someone or something for who or what it really is. Expect the weighty, heavy glory of God to invade your life, devastate your enemies, and deliver you from your depression and fear. Believe it! Expect Him to be recognized in your life—His glory is coming to you!

Expect light to shine on your path.

Isaiah 60:2–3 communicates that light will overcome darkness. Look for the light of understanding to come where you have been confused. As you read and meditate on Scripture, expect to receive revelation. The light of God that grows brighter and brighter until the full day is going to shine on your path. (See Proverbs 4:18.) No longer will you walk in the darkness of hope deferred, groping to find your way. You are coming into a season of light. Expect it!

Expect His presence to be evident in your life in a new way.

Isaiah 60:2 says that "the LORD will rise upon you." If you have grown cold or lukewarm in your walk with God, expect His presence to awaken you to a new season of intimacy. Expect a fresh passion for the Lord to be ignited within you. Anticipate visitations from Him in the night hours. In your quiet times with Him, look for the reality of who He is to explode off the pages of His Word. Expect His presence to overwhelm you.

Expect new vision to come to you.

Isaiah 60:4 states, "Lift up your eyes round about and see; they all gather together, they come to you. Your sons will come from afar, and your daughters will be carried in the arms." This is a day for renewed vision. If you, like Moses and Abraham, have suffered from hope deferred and lost your vision, expect new vision to explode in you. Look! It is not a time for retreat, apathy, hopelessness, or stagnation. Take hold of a fresh ability to see ahead as never before.

Isaiah was prophesying future events, challenging them to see *by faith.* Jesus said in John 4:35, "Lift up your eyes and look on the fields, that they are white for harvest." He was telling them to look *by faith.* Elijah said he heard the "sound of abundance of rain" before there was ever a cloud in the sky (1 Kings

18:41, KJV). Begin to see with your eyes of faith in this new season. Stir up your expectations—new vision is about to burst forth!

Expect new joy to rise up in you.

"Then you shall see and be radiant, and your heart shall thrill and tremble with joy [at the glorious deliverance] and be enlarged" (Isa. 60:5, AMP). The Hebrew word translated "thrill" means to "tremble or palpitate." You are going to be so excited as hope wells up within you that your heart is going to race! Your diseased heart is being healed to such an extent that it will have the capacity to rejoice. Expect the joy of the Lord to become your strength (Neh. 8:10). Deliverance is coming to you, and instead of oppression you will have joy. You are being healed of hope deferred, and joy is going to overwhelm you. Expect it!

Expect the favor of the Lord to come to you.

Isaiah 60:10 says, "In My favor I have had compassion on you." Expect favor wherever you are—in your job, family, church, marriage, business endeavors, community—every place you go. Jesus came "to proclaim the favorable year of the Lord" (Luke 4:19). Look for His favor to open doors for you, to bring the contacts you need, and to prepare the way before you. Expect the favor of the Lord in all your relationships.

* * * *

The next list of "expects" is gleaned from Peter's hope-deferred jail time in Acts 12. This was during a time of tremendous prosperity as well as great persecution in the early church. Wonderful things were happening spiritually, and yet Herod had begun to attack them. He had killed James, the brother of John; then he arrested Peter, putting him in prison, with plans to execute him as well. The church prayed fervently for Peter's release, and he had a dramatic visitation from an angel who delivered him from prison. Here are several expectations taken from this powerful chapter.

Expect angelic visitations.

"And behold, an angel of the Lord suddenly appeared" (Acts 12:7). I don't necessarily mean you will literally see angels, although you may—but expect them, however, to fulfill in your life what the Scriptures say angels do. Expect protection—they will bear you up in their arms, protecting you (Ps. 91:11–12). Anticipate their encampment around you (Ps. 34:7). Look for angelic visits to bring healing and provision into your life. And, yes, expect them to invade your prison of hope-deferred bondage and deliver you. Expect your mountain of Horeb to rumble and shake with the presence of God and angelic visitors.

Expect a light to shine in your prison.

"And a light shone in the cell" (Acts 12:7). Expect your night to give way to the dawn. I once heard a good friend, Pastor Lon Stokes, share from this passage. He connected it to Genesis chapter 1 and the significance of God beginning each day of creation with darkness. Expect the Holy Spirit to hover over the darkness of your hope-deferred night and create a new day of hope, just as He did in Genesis 1. Expect a light to shine in your cell of despair, transforming your surroundings. Expect the light of hope to break forth as the dawn!

Expect your chains to fall off.

Scripture says of Peter, "And his chains fell off his hands" (Acts 12:7). You have the right to freedom. Hope deferred is beginning to yield to victory. This is a day of breakthrough. Believe it. If you've been enslaved to sin, this is your hour to be free. If you've been held captive by oppression, discouragement, and depression, this is your point of release. If you've been imprisoned with disease, this is your time to be healed. If you've been bound with hopelessness, this is your day to hope. Expect your chains to fall off! The demoniacs in Matthew 8:28–32 were hopelessly bound in an impossible condition, yet Jesus delivered them in a moment. Expect breakthrough.

Expect your prison doors to open.

"Peter followed him out of the prison" (Acts 12:9, NIV). You are going to be free. Jesus came to release you from the prison of hope deferred. Luke 4:18 states, "He has sent me to proclaim freedom for the prisoners" (NIV). You are walking out of the captivity that has kept you bound and into a new place of freedom. Tell your heart to start beating again. It's time to get busy livin'!

Expect gates to open.

"They came to the iron gate that leads into the city, which opened for them by itself" (Acts 12:10). In Scripture gates often symbolize authority. Expect the authority of the Lord to be released into your life. You will possess the gate of your enemy (Gen. 22:17). The gates of hell will no longer prevail against you (Matt. 16:18). The King of glory is coming into your city, your home, your family, and your life (Ps. 24:7–9). Expect the gate of hope to open!

Expect your enemies to fall.

"And immediately an angel of the Lord struck [Herod]" (Acts 12:23). Herod, who had thrown Peter in jail, was stricken and died. Of course, this expectation does not refer to people but to the enemies of your soul. The strongholds associated with hope deferred in your life will come down. The enemies that have tried to imprison you are going to be defeated. "Let God arise, let His enemies be scattered, and let those who hate Him flee before Him" (Ps. 68:1).

Expect the Word of the Lord to grow and be multiplied.

"But the word of God grew and multiplied" (Acts 12:24, KJV). Expect the Word of the Lord to prosper in you. Expect the Word of the Lord over your city and nation to increase and be fulfilled. Expect every promise from Scripture to come to pass in your life. Hope in God's Word. Expect it to grow and multiply. "The LORD will command His lovingkindness in the daytime; and His song will be with [you] in the night" (Ps. 42:8). The God of hope will fill you with all joy and peace in believing, and you will abound in hope (Rom. 15:13)!

A life filled with hope is your destiny and inheritance as one of God's kids. Don't settle for anything less. Remember Bartimaeus in Mark 10? He was determined to receive his sight. When he knew his healing was within range, this man shouted out, "Jesus, Son of David, have mercy on me!" (v. 47). People around him insisted that he be quiet, but he didn't care what people were saying—nothing was going to keep him from his miracle. He refused to give up, and he received his healing.

In Luke 5 a paralyzed man determined not to miss

his miracle, even though it didn't seem possible to get to Jesus. His friends took him "up on the roof and let him down through the tiles with his stretcher, into the middle of the crowd, in front of Jesus" (v. 19), and he was made whole. Like this overcomer, be tenacious! Refuse to live in the state of hope deferred. Do whatever is necessary to receive your breakthrough.

> *A life filled with hope is your destiny and inheritance as one of God's kids. Don't settle for anything less.*

Expect your heart to get well. Expect the clouds of doubt to yield to the dawn of hope. Expect a new beginning in your life. Expect to enjoy life again. Expect to win.

Expect!

REFLECT on the Power of Hope

A life filled with the power of hope is your destiny and inheritance as one of God's kids.

For there is hope for a tree, when it is cut down, that it will sprout again, and its shoots will not fail. Though its roots grow old in the ground and its stump dies in the dry soil, at the scent of water it will flourish and put forth sprigs like a plant.

—Job 14:7–9

APPLY the Power of Hope

Throughout this chapter seeds of hope and faith were planted within you. Continue to plant more of these seeds on the now fertile soil of your heart by using this chapter as an ongoing prayer declaration and Bible study guide. Allow God to continually water those seeds with His healing presence, listening for His messages of hope whispered in response to your devotion. In doing so, you will cultivate a joyful expectation of all the good things God is working out on your behalf.

PRAY the Power of Hope

Father, in Your compassion, You've promised to cause new life to spring forth even from the barren recesses of my hopeless heart. I am extremely grateful for Your unfailing love and faithfulness, which have preserved me. Because of Your tender mercies, my forgotten dreams will flourish once again. Even though I walk through death's valley, I will not fear. I choose to walk by faith, anchoring myself to the assurance of things hoped for and the conviction of things unseen. In You, Jesus, I will have victory over my enemies. I will eat from the tree of life. I will partake of hope fulfilled!

SCRIPTURES TO READ: Job 14:7–9; Hebrews 10:39; 11:1; 2 Corinthians 4:18; 5:7; Proverbs 13:12; Revelation 2:7; Psalm 23; 40:11; Isaiah 59; 60

CHAPTER 1–GET BUSY LIVIN'

CHAPTER 2–YOU WILL CROW AGAIN

_____

_____

_____

_____

_____

_____

_____

_____

_____

_____

_____

_____

_____

CHAPTER 3–FACE THE WIND

_____

_____

_____

_____

_____

_____

_____

_____

_____

_____

_____

_____

CHAPTER 4—LAUGHTER IS COMING

_____

_____

_____

_____

_____

_____

_____

_____

_____

_____

_____

_____

CHAPTER 5—THERE IS MUSIC IN YOU STILL

_____

_____

_____

_____

_____

_____

_____

_____

_____

_____

_____

_____

_____

CHAPTER 6—WINTER IS OVER

_____

_____

_____

_____

_____

_____

_____

_____

_____

_____

_____

_____

_____

Chapter 7–Tell Your Heart to Beat Again

CHAPTER 8–MINING THE GOLD

_____

_____

_____

_____

_____

_____

_____

_____

_____

_____

_____

_____

_____

_____

CHAPTER 9–FRESH START MOUNTAIN

_____

_____

_____

_____

_____

_____

_____

_____

_____

_____

_____

_____

CHAPTER 10–THE STAFF OF GOD

_____

_____

_____

_____

_____

_____

_____

_____

_____

_____

_____

_____

CHAPTER 11–THE HOLY PLACE

_____

_____

_____

_____

_____

_____

_____

_____

_____

_____

_____

_____

CHAPTER 12–EXPECT!

_____

_____

_____

_____

_____

_____

_____

_____

_____

_____

_____

_____

_____

NOTES

INTRODUCTION

1. Emily Dickinson, *The Poems of Emily Dickinson*, R. W. Franklin, ed. (Cambridge, MA: Harvard University Press, 1999), poem #314.

CHAPTER 1
GET BUSY LIVIN'

1. Jack Canfield, Mark Victor Hansen, and Barry Spilchuk, compilers, *A Cup of Chicken Soup for the Soul* (Deerfield Beach FL: Health Communications, Inc., 1996), 209.
2. *The Shawshank Redemption*, directed by Frank Darabont (Hollywood, CA: Castle Rock Entertainment, 1994), DVD. While the television broadcast of this movie was edited, I understand the movie itself contains inappropriate language and activities. Thus I would not want anyone to misconstrue my referring to it as a recommendation of the unedited version of the movie.
3. Mark Hamer, Mika Kivimaki, Avijit Lahiri, Michael G. Marmot, and Andrew Steptoe, "Persistent Cognitive Depressive Symptoms Associated With Coronary Calcification," *Atherosclerosis* 210, no. 1 (May 2010): 209–213, http://www.ncbi.nlm.nih.gov/pmc/articles/PMC2877780/ (accessed October 1, 2013).
4. *New York Times*, "Despair and Risk of Artery Disease," September 3, 1997, http://www.nytimes.com/1997/09/03/us/despair-and-risk-of-artery-disease.html (accessed October 1, 2013).
5. Tom C. Russ, Emmanuel Stamatakis, Mark Hamer, John M. Starr, Mika Kivimaki, and G. David Batty,

"Association Between Psychological Distress and Mortality: Individual Participant Pooled Analysis of 10 Prospective Cohort Studies," *British Medical Journal* 345 (July 31, 2012): e4933, http://www.bmj.com/ content/345/bmj.e4933 (accessed October 1, 2013).

CHAPTER 2
YOU WILL CROW AGAIN

1. McKinley Irvin, "32 Shocking Divorce Statistics," October 30, 2012, http://www.mckinleyirvin.com/ blog/divorce/32-shocking-divorce-statistics/ (accessed October 1, 2013).
2. Ibid.
3. Ibid.
4. Statistics from various government agencies, as related in Felicia Ann Tralongo, "Children and Divorce," PsychologicalAssociates.com, http://www .psychologicalassoc.com/Children%20and%20Divorce .html (accessed October 1, 2013).
5. National Institute of Mental Health, "The Numbers Count: Mental Disorders in America," http://www .nimh.nih.gov/health/publications/the-numbers-count -mental-disorders-in-America/index.shtml#Kessler Prevalence (accessed October 1, 2013).
6. Centers for Disease Control and Prevention (CDC), "Suicide Prevention: Youth Suicide," August 15, 2012, http://www.cdc.gov/violenceprevention/pub/youth_ suicide.html (accessed October 1, 2013).
7. National Institute of Mental Health, "Many Teens Considering Suicide Do Not Receive Specialized Mental Health Care," October 12, 2012, http://www .nimh.nih.gov/news/science-news/2012/many-teens -considering-suicide-do-not-receive-specialized-mental -health-care.shtml (accessed October 2, 2013).

8. Lola Butcher, "The Mental Health Crisis," *Hospitals and Health Networks*, May 2012, http://www.hhnmag.com/hhnmag/jsp/articledisplay.jsp?dcrpath=HHNMAG/Article/data/05MAY2012/0512HHN_Coverstory&domain=HHNMAG (accessed October 2, 2013).

9. Ryan C. Perry, "Ministry Lends Ear to Struggling Pastors," *News-Journal* (Longview, TX), May 26, 2012, http://www.news-journal.com/features/religion/ministry-lends-ear-to-struggling-pastors/article_a687d2db-980d-58af-bcc3-4f60be62a2cb.html (accessed October 2, 2013).

10. Ivan Charles Blake, "Pastor for Life," *Ministry*, July/August 2010, https://www.ministrymagazine.org/archive/2010/07-august/pastor-for-life (accessed October 2, 2013).

11. MaranathaLife.com, "Maranatha Life's Life-Line for Pastors: Statistics About Pastors," http://maranathalife.com/lifeline/stats.htm (accessed October 2, 2013).

12. Perry, "Ministry Lends Ear to Struggling Pastors."

13. Marilyn B. Oden, *100 Meditations on Hope* (Nashville: Upper Room Books, 1995), 11.

14. As related in Craig Brian Larson, ed., *750 Engaging Illustrations for Preachers, Teachers, and Writers* (Grand Rapids, MI: Baker Books, 2007), 411–412.

Chapter 3
Face the Wind

1. Curtis Vaughan, ed., *The Word: The Bible From Twenty-Six Translations* (Atlanta, GA: Mathis Publishers, 1993).

2. As quoted in Bruce Bickel and Stan Jantz, *God Is in the Small Stuff* (Uhrichsville, OH: Barbour Publishing, 1998), chapter 19.

3. As quoted in Daniel Kurtzman, "John Kennedy Quotes," About.com Political Humor, http://political humor.about.com/od/Funny-Presidential-Quotes/a/ John-Kennedy-Quotes.htm (accessed October 2, 2013).
4. Robert J. Morgan, *Real Stories for the Soul* (Nashville: Thomas Nelson, 2000), 120–121.
5. Larson, ed., *750 Engaging Illustrations for Preachers, Teachers, and Writers*, 457.

CHAPTER 4
LAUGHTER IS COMING

1. "My Hope Is Built" by Edward Mote. Public domain.
2. Oden, *100 Meditations on Hope*, 25.
3. Morgan, *Real Stories for the Soul*, 53–55.

CHAPTER 5
THERE IS MUSIC IN YOU STILL

1. Jack Canfield, Mark Victor Hansen, and Heather McNamara, *Chicken Soup for the Unsinkable Soul* (Deerfield Beach, FL: Health Communications, Inc., 1999), 58.
2. Spiros Zodhiates, *The Complete Word Study Dictionary* (Iowa Falls, IA: Word Bible Publishers, Inc., 1992), 570.
3. Oden, *100 Meditations on Hope*, 72.
4. Spiros Zodhiates, ed., *Hebrew-Greek Key Study Bible— New American Standard,* rev. ed. (Chattanooga, TN: AMG Publishers, 1990), 1785.
5. Canfield, Hansen, and McNamara, *Chicken Soup for the Unsinkable Soul*, 142–143.
6. About.com, "Wilma Rudolph Quotes," Women's History, http://womenshistory.about.com/od/quotes/a/ wilma_rudolph.htm (accessed October 2, 2013).

7. M. B. Roberts, "Rudolph Ran and World Went Wild," ESPN.com, http://espn.go.com/sportscentury/features/00016444.html (accessed October 2, 2013).
8. Adapted from Morgan, *Real Stories for the Soul*, 117–119.

CHAPTER 6
WINTER IS OVER

1. Zodhiates, *Hebrew-Greek Key Study Bible—New American Standard*, 1716.
2. Ibid.
3. James Strong, *The New Strong's Exhaustive Concordance of the Bible* (Nashville: Thomas Nelson Publishers, 1990), s.v. OT:5158, "*nachal.*"
4. Dictionary.com, *Collins English Dictionary— Complete & Unabridged 10th Edition* (New York: HarperCollins Publishers, s.v. "synergism," http://dictionary.reference.com/cite.html?qh=synergism&ia=ced (accessed October 2, 2013).
5. Adapted from Edward K. Powell, *Fresh Illustrations for Preaching and Teaching* (Grand Rapids, MI: Baker Book House, 1997), 118.
6. Adapted from Ted Kyle and John Todd, *A Treasury of Bible Illustrations* (Chattanooga, TN: AMG Publishers, 1995), 215.

CHAPTER 7
TELL YOUR HEART TO BEAT AGAIN

1. Charles Bracelen Flood, *Lee: The Last Years* (New York: Houghton Mifflin, 1981), 136.
2. Rubem Alves, as quoted in *Spiritual Literacy: Reading the Sacred in Everyday Life,* comp. Frederic and Mary

Ann Brussat (New York: Simon and Schuster, 1996), 194.

3. While this can be found on many Internet sites, the author is unknown.

4. Spiros Zodhiates, *Illustrations of Bible Truths* (Chattanooga, TN: AMG Publishers, 1995), 267.

5. Craig Brian Larson, *Contemporary Illustrations for Preachers, Teachers, and Writers* (Grand Rapids MI: Baker Book House, 1996), 110.

6. Adapted from Larson, ed., *750 Engaging Illustrations for Preachers, Teachers, and Writers*, 31–32.

CHAPTER 8
MINING THE GOLD

1. Rich DeVos, *Hope From My Heart* (Nashville: Thomas Nelson Publishers, 2000), 27, 33.

2. Zodhiates, *Hebrew-Greek Key Study Bible—New American Standard*, 1756.

3. Ibid.

4. Canfield, Hansen, and Spilchuk, *A Cup of Chicken Soup for the Soul*, 76–77.

CHAPTER 9
FRESH START MOUNTAIN

1. *Miracles Happen When Women Pray* by Bobbye Byerly, pp. 40–45. Copyright © 2002, Gospel Light/Regal Books, Ventura, CA 93003. Used by permission.

CHAPTER 10
THE STAFF OF GOD

1. Alice Gray, *More Stories for the Heart* (Sisters, OR: Multnomah Publishers, Inc., 1997), 247.

2. Strong, *The New Strong's Exhaustive Concordance of the Bible*, s.v. OT:4294, *"matteh."*
3. Adapted from Neil T. Anderson, *Victory Over the Darkness* (Ventura, CA: Regal Books, 2000), 89–90.
4. Adapted from Sandy Dengler, *Susanna Wesley, Servant of God* (Chicago: Moody Press, 1987).

CHAPTER 11
THE HOLY PLACE

1. Adapted from *The Best of Catherine Marshall*, ed. by Leonard E. LeSourd (Ada, MI: Chosen Books, 1993). Permission requested.
2. Gray, *More Stories for the Heart*, 220.

Scott Foeller
+603-453-0145

Made in the USA
Columbia, SC
08 May 2022